United States Government Accountability Office

Report to the Chairman, Committee on the Budget, House of Representatives

I0416902

September 2013

BUDGET ISSUES

Key Questions to Consider When Evaluating Balances in Federal Accounts

September 2013

BUDGET ISSUES

Key Questions to Consider When Evaluating Balances in Federal Accounts

GAO Highlights

Highlights of GAO-13-798, a report to the Chairman, Committee on the Budget, House of Representatives

Why GAO Did This Study

Given the fiscal pressures facing the nation, examination of balances carried forward into future fiscal years (carryover balances) provides an opportunity to identify areas where the federal government can improve and maximize the use of resources. GAO was asked to review issues related to federal carryover balances. GAO's objectives were to (1) identify key questions for congressional committees, managers, and other reviewers to consider when evaluating carryover balances, including whether to reduce them, and (2) describe how answering these key questions provides insight into why carryover balances may exist in selected accounts.

GAO reviewed carryover balances from fiscal years 2007 through 2012 in eight selected accounts from the Departments of Defense (DOD), Health and Human Services (HHS), Housing and Urban Development (HUD), and Treasury. Account selection was based on several characteristics, including the average size of the balance, budget function, type of account, agency, and whether the account was composed of mandatory or discretionary funds.

GAO is not making any recommendations. DOD, HHS, HUD, and Treasury generally agreed with our findings and provided technical comments that were incorporated as appropriate. HHS provided comments stating that conclusions drawn from the report may not apply across the board to all accounts.

View GAO-13-798. For more information, contact Susan J. Irving, Director for Federal Budget Analysis, (202) 512-6806 or irvings@gao.gov.

What GAO Found

Carryover balances in fiscal year 2012 were $2.2 trillion, of which about $800 billion had not yet been obligated. Answering key questions during review of carryover balances provides insights into why a balance exists, what size balance is appropriate, and what opportunities (if any) for savings exist. Given that a single account may support a single program or multiple programs—or that multiple accounts may support a single program—these questions can be applied when evaluating balances at either the account or program level. Examination of balances may assist decision makers in identifying opportunities to achieve budgetary savings or redirecting resources to other priorities. However, the complexity of the federal budget is such that a case-by-case analysis is needed to understand how best to achieve these financial benefits.

What mission and goals is the account or program supporting? Understanding the mission activities, goals, and programs the account supports provides information about whether a program needs to maintain a balance to operate smoothly, what size balance is appropriate, and whether opportunities for savings exist. Accounts GAO reviewed maintained balances to support activities such as long-term acquisition of military aircraft and public health emergency preparedness.

What are the sources and fiscal characteristics of the funding? The sources and fiscal characteristics of the funding present different issues in changing the size of carryover balances. Accounts such as Treasury's Exchange Stabilization Fund, receive "such sums as may be necessary" and may require programmatic changes to effectively reduce balances. In such cases, simply reducing balances may have no economic benefit and could impose unnecessary administrative costs. If funds are discretionary, such as with HUD's Homeless Assistance Grants, balances can be controlled through appropriations acts.

What factors affect the size or composition of the carryover balances? Understanding factors within and outside an agency's control that affect its "spendout rate" provides insight to the composition of the carryover balance as a whole. Funds in accounts that support activities such as certain procurement or disaster relief may be obligated fairly quickly, but are expended over a longer period as milestones are met or as grantees draw down funds. Accounts with quick spendout rates, such as those that provide cash payments to government-sponsored enterprises, disburse funds soon after obligation.

How does the agency estimate and manage carryover balances? Understanding an agency's processes for estimating and managing balances provides information to assess how effectively agencies anticipate program needs and ensure the most efficient use of resources. For the mandatory accounts GAO reviewed, such as the Federal Housing Administration's Mutual Mortgage Insurance Capital Reserve account, agencies focused on future needs of the account and relied on economic indicators and historical trends to estimate future balances. For discretionary accounts GAO reviewed, such as the U.S. Army Corps of Engineers' Construction account, agencies used historical data combined with current variables to estimate carryover balances.

United States Government Accountability Office

Contents

Figures

Abbreviations

APA	Aircraft Procurement, Army
CDBG	Community Development Block Grant
CDF	Community Development Fund
Corps	U.S. Army Corps of Engineers
CR	continuing resolution
DOD	Department of Defense
DOT	Department of Transportation
ESF	Exchange Stabilization Fund
Fannie Mae	Federal National Mortgage Association
FDIC	Federal Deposit Insurance Corporation
FHA	Federal Housing Administration
FHFA	Federal Housing Finance Agency
Freddie Mac	Federal Home Loan Mortgage Corporation
GSE	Government Sponsored Enterprise
HAG	Homeless Assistance Grants
HERA	Housing and Economic Recovery Act
HHS	Department of Health and Human Services
HUD	Department of Housing and Urban Development
IMF	International Monetary Fund
MMI Fund	Mutual Mortgage Insurance Fund
NSP	Neighborhood Stabilization Program
NSSE	National Special Security Events
OMB	Office of Management and Budget
PHSSEF	Public Health and Social Services Emergency Fund
SDR	Special Drawing Rights
TARP	Troubled Asset Relief Program
Treasury	Department of the Treasury
USSGL	U.S. Standard General Ledger

September 30, 2013

The Honorable Paul Ryan
Chairman
Committee on the Budget
House of Representatives

Dear Mr. Ryan,

Given the fiscal pressures facing the nation, the need to identify opportunities for savings, find ways to better leverage resources, and increase accountability has become even more critical to the success of federal agencies and the programs they administer. Congress needs pertinent and reliable information to adequately assess agencies' progress and to ensure accountability for results. One area that managers and other decision makers look to when seeking potential savings are carryover balances: balances in individual agency accounts that are carried forward into future fiscal years. Carryover balances amounted to $2.2 trillion in fiscal year 2012, of which almost $800 billion had not yet been obligated.[1] Examination of these balances may assist decision makers in identifying opportunities to achieve budgetary savings or in redirecting resources toward other priorities. However, the complexity of the federal budget is such that a case-by-case analysis is needed to understand how best to achieve these financial benefits.

You asked us to review the size and management of carryover balances in various types of appropriations accounts. Our objectives were to: (1) identify key questions to consider when evaluating carryover balances, including whether to reduce them, and (2) describe how answering these key questions provides insight into why carryover balances existed in selected accounts during fiscal years 2007 through 2012, and how agencies estimated and managed these balances. In addition, we analyzed the size and composition of carryover balances in the federal budget from fiscal years 2007 through 2012. This information is provided in appendix I.

---

[1] An obligation is a definite commitment that creates a legal liability of the government for the payment of goods and services ordered or received, or a legal duty on the part of the United States that could mature into a legal liability by virtue of actions of another party.

Background

Although federal funding may be available to obligate for one-year, multiple years, or until expended (no-year), only accounts with multi-year or no-year funds may carry over amounts that remain legally available for new obligations from one fiscal year to the next. Carryover balances are composed of two elements: (1) unobligated funds and (2) obligated funds for which payment has not yet been made. While attention is focused on the unobligated portion, looking at both elements provides a fuller reflection of what is happening in an account. It also provides insights into opportunities for potential budgetary savings.

Federal spending is categorized as "discretionary" or "mandatory." This distinction refers to the way budget authority is provided. Discretionary spending is controlled through annual appropriations acts (plus in some cases supplemental appropriations acts), which may provide multi-year or no-year funds.[2] Under certain legal authorities, some discretionary accounts are funded entirely, or in part, through the collection of user fees, interagency transactions, or dedicated excise taxes. Specifically, the level of discretionary funding in an account is provided by, and controlled through, the annual appropriations process.

In contrast, mandatory spending accounts, which include "entitlements," receive budget authority through laws other than appropriations acts. Many mandatory programs receive budget authority for an unspecified amount made available as the result of previously enacted legislation, with no need for further legislative action. For example, Medicare, veterans' pensions, Social Security, and federal crop insurance are mandatory programs. By statute, funding to these programs is driven by eligibility rules and benefit formulas, which means that funds are made available as needed to provide benefits to those who are eligible and wish to participate. Over the last several years, mandatory accounts have represented an increasing share of total unobligated balances across the federal government.

Figure 1 shows how budget authority is provided and how authorized funds may accumulate, ultimately leading to a carryover balance.

---

[2] Funds are available for obligation on a one-year, multi-year, or no-year (until expended) basis. Such time limitations are referred to as the period of availability.

Figure 1: Overview of How an Account Accumulates a Carryover Balance

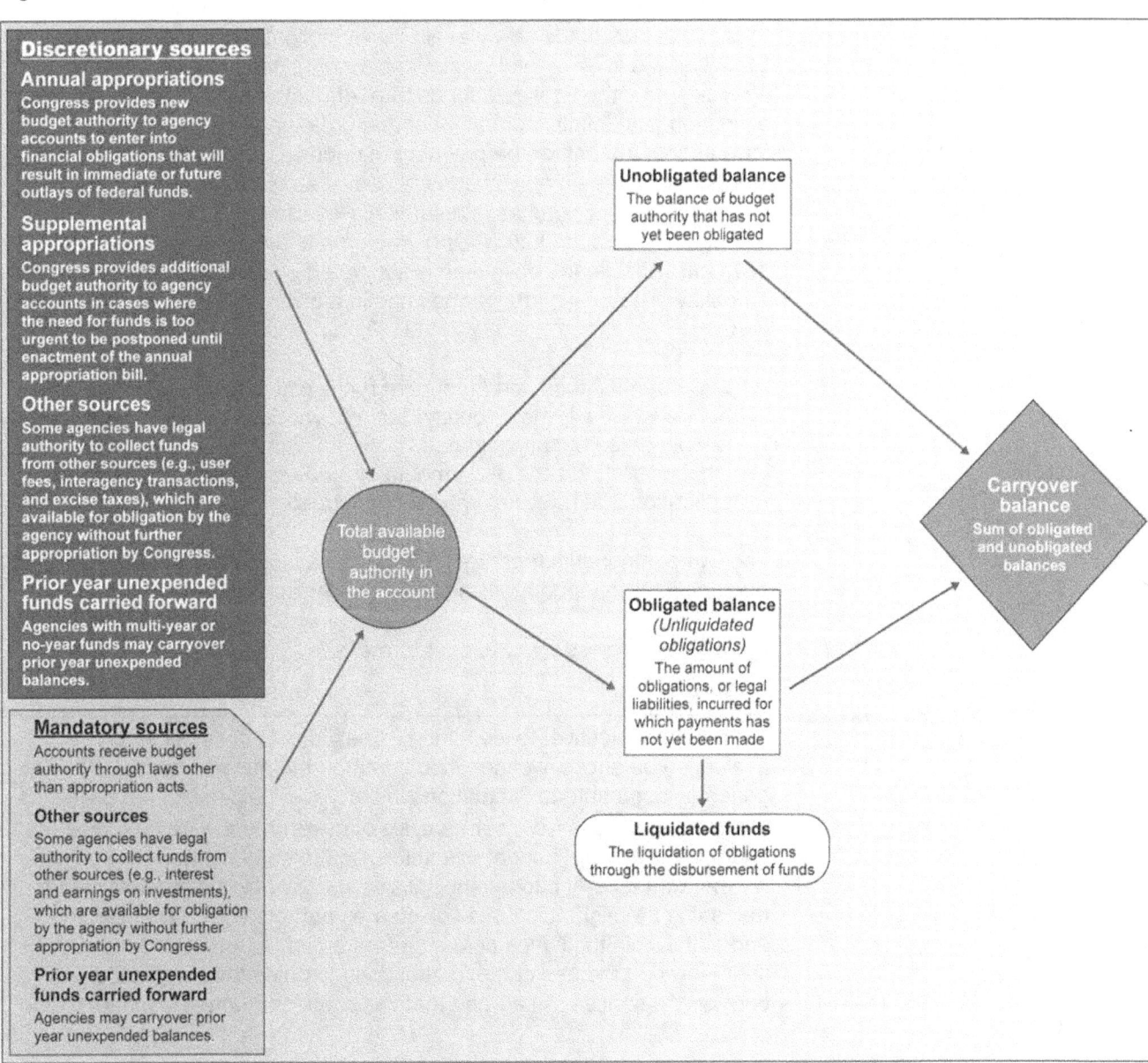

Source: GAO.

In any given year, the total budgetary resources available in an account consist of unobligated funds carried forward from previous years, if applicable, plus funds newly available for obligation in that fiscal year. Based on the level of total available budget authority in the account, agencies may then obligate funds throughout the fiscal year. An obligation is a definite commitment that creates a legal liability of the federal government for the payment of goods and services. For example, an agency incurs an obligation when it places an order, signs a contract, awards a grant or purchases a service. Payment may be made immediately or in the future. Only when funds are actually disbursed for payment—that is, the obligation is liquidated—does an obligation become an outlay. The total carryover balance in a given account consists of two parts:

- Obligated balance: the amount of funds which have been obligated but for which payment (outlay) has not yet been made; these funds are obligated but unliquidated.
- Unobligated balance: the amount of funds still legally available for obligation that have not yet been obligated.

The two components represent different phases of budget execution and present different opportunities for budgetary savings.

For a detailed glossary of budget terms, see appendix V.

Objectives, Scope, and Methodology

For our first objective, to identify key questions to consider when evaluating balances, we identified common themes and factors that generally contribute to fluctuations in carryover balances.[3] We developed the list of questions from our analysis of government-wide guidance on budget preparation, budget execution, and internal controls. In addition, we met with federal budget specialists, agency officials responsible for managing the eight accounts selected as part of our second objective, and staff within the Office of Management and Budget (OMB) to obtain their views on the use of these questions to guide the examination of carryover balances. All agreed that the questions were reasonable. Our

---

[3] For the purpose of this report, we focused on multi-year and no-year accounts where the unobligated balance is carried forward and is legally available for new obligations. We did not focus on the unobligated balance of fiscal year funds that are in expired status and generally are not available for new obligations.

prior work on federal budgeting, user fees, budget triggers, and managing under continuing resolutions also informed the development of the key questions.

Our second objective was to describe how answering these key questions provides information about why carryover balances were reported in selected accounts during fiscal years 2007 through 2012, and how agencies estimated and managed these balances. To do this, we selected a nongeneralizable sample of eight accounts with multi-year or no-year funds to use as case illustrations. To start our selection process, we collected and compared end-of-year actual unexpired unobligated balances plus obligated balances for which payment had not yet been made. We queried this data from OMB's MAX database for all accounts in the federal budget for fiscal years 2007 through 2012. We found the data to be sufficiently reliable for the purpose of our report.[4] We identified the 100 accounts with the largest average unobligated balance during fiscal years 2007 through 2012.[5] From that list of 100 accounts, we selected eight accounts representing a variety of characteristics, including the size of the average unobligated balance, budget function, type of account, agency, and whether the account was composed of mandatory funds, discretionary funds, or a combination of both. We reviewed the selected agencies' estimates as they were reported in the President's Budget Appendices for fiscal years 2007 through 2012. Table 1 lists the selected accounts. For the purpose of this report, we did not seek to identify specific savings related to the selected accounts.

---

[4] To determine the reliability of the data, the team cross-checked the MAX data against the numbers reported in the corresponding President's Budget Appendices. Data reported in MAX and the Budget Appendix are subject to rigorous review and checks through OMB to help ensure consistency of the data. Accordingly, such data were considered reliable for the purpose of this report.

[5] Although the period over which we reviewed the accounts is fiscal years 2007 through 2012, at the time that we chose our nongeneralizable sample, actual data for 2012 was not yet available. Therefore, our selection of accounts was based on data from fiscal years 2007 through 2011. We included the size of the average unobligated balance as one of the selection criteria because it is the portion of the balance that frequently raises questions.

Table 1: Case Illustration Accounts

Dollars in Billions

Account name and department	Designation	Budget subfunction	Average unobligated balance, fiscal years 2007-2012
Government Sponsored Enterprise Preferred Stock Purchase Agreements (Dept. of the Treasury)	Mandatory	Mortgage Credit, 371	$239.95
Exchange Stabilization Fund (Dept. of the Treasury)	Mandatory	International Financial Programs, 155	$48.23
Federal Housing Administration-Mutual Mortgage Insurance Capital Reserve (Dept. of Housing and Urban Development)	Mandatory	Mortgage Credit, 371	$10.74
U.S. Army Corps of Engineers-Civil Works, Construction (Dept. of Defense)	Discretionary	Water Resources, 301	$4.32
Community Development Fund (Dept. of Housing and Urban Development)	Split	Community Development, 451	$4.27
Public Health and Social Services Emergency Fund (Dept. of Health and Human Services)	Discretionary	Health Care Services, 551	$3.35
Army Aircraft Procurement (Dept. of Defense)	Discretionary	Dept of Defense-Military, 051	$2.65
Homeless Assistance Grants (Dept. of Housing and Urban Development)	Discretionary	Housing Assistance, 604	$1.97

Source: GAO analysis of OMB MAX data.

Note: Split accounts contain both mandatory and discretionary funds.

Although these eight accounts represent less than 1 percent of the total number of accounts in the federal budget, they represent approximately 34 percent of unobligated balances across the federal government. To determine what factors contributed to carryover balances in these accounts and how the selected agencies managed them, we reviewed agency budget reports and guidance, congressional budget justifications, and financial and annual reports. We also interviewed agency officials to obtain their explanations and discuss the practices and procedures they use to estimate and manage balances.

We conducted our review from November 2012 through September 2013 in accordance with generally accepted government auditing standards. Those standards require that we plan and perform the audit to obtain sufficient, appropriate evidence to provide a reasonable basis for our findings and conclusions based on our audit objectives. We believe that the evidence obtained provides a reasonable basis for our findings and conclusions based on our audit objectives.

Four Key Questions to Consider When Evaluating Carryover Balances

To assist congressional and agency-level decision makers as well as other reviewers in their evaluation of agencies' carryover balances, we identified four overarching key questions to consider:

- What mission and goals is the account or program supporting?
- What are the sources and fiscal characteristics of the funding?
- What factors affect the size or composition of the carryover balance?
- How does the agency estimate and manage carryover balances?

Each of the four key questions leads to a set of second-tier, more specific questions that can help frame the analysis of carryover balances. Answering each of the four overarching questions and their second-tier questions provides insight into why a carryover balance exists, what size balance is appropriate, and what opportunities, if any, for savings exist. In addition, it may provide opportunities for enhanced oversight of agencies' management of federal funds and identify areas where the federal government can improve and maximize its use of resources. These questions can be applied when evaluating carryover balances at either the account or program level. A single account may support a single program or multiple programs. Conversely, a single program may be supported by multiple accounts. Further, the balance in a single year may reflect events particular to that year and so present an incomplete or possibly misleading view of what is happening in a given account or program over time. Therefore, a longer view is preferable.

Since the many accounts that make up the federal budget vary greatly and individual accounts have their own unique characteristics, we do not suggest that the following set of questions represents all the questions that could be considered when evaluating carryover balances. As congressional committees, managers, and other reviewers apply these evaluative questions, additional questions may arise. In some cases, however, a few of the questions may provide sufficient information to understand the nature of the balance. The following sections discuss the questions in more detail. In addition, all of the questions are presented as an evaluative guide in appendix II.

What Mission and Goals Is the Account or Program Supporting?

Understanding the mission activities, goals,[6] and programs the account supports provides information about whether a program needs to maintain a balance to operate smoothly, what size balance is appropriate, and whether opportunities for savings exist. Such context can inform assessments of whether, and how, to reduce carryover balances and what effect a reduction would have on the agency's ability to carry out its mission. For example, an account established to provide stability in the financial or housing market needs a balance to ensure the agency has sufficient resources to respond quickly to adverse events. Similarly, we have previously reported on agency intragovernmental revolving funds for which a balance is needed to maintain price stability for customer agencies or to ensure that the providing agency has funding available to complete services or work being performed for customer agencies that cross fiscal years.[7]

Examples of specific questions to understand how the mission affects balances include

- What are the primary mission and goals the account or program is intended to achieve?
- What is the nature and purpose of the balance and how does it support the mission and goals (e.g., counter economic crisis, sustain business-like activities, emergency funding needs)?
- Have there been changes to the program or mission that may affect balances (e.g., additional responsibilities, major reorganization)?
- What type of activity (e.g., grants, procurement, direct services) is the account used for to achieve the agency's mission and goals? What are the implications of carryover balances?
- What programs are funded by the account and how much does each contribute, if at all, to the carryover balance (i.e., does a large portion of the balance result from any particular programs)?
- Is it a new account or program or have the program goals and objectives changed? How has this affected the agency's ability to obligate funds?

---

[6] Agencies are required to develop long-term and annual goals and measure and report on progress towards those goals on an annual basis. This is a requirement under the Government Performance Results Act of 1993, (GPRA), Pub. L. No. 103-62, 107 Stat. 285 (1993), which was recently amended and expanded by the GPRA Modernization Act of 2010, Pub. L. No. 111-352, 124 Stat. 3866 (2011). GAO, *Managing for Results: Opportunities for Congress to Address Government Performance Issues*, GAO-12-215R (Washington, D.C.: Dec. 9, 2011). Also see GAO, *Managing for Results: Executive Branch Should More Fully Implement the GPRA Modernization Act to Address Pressing Government Challenges*, GAO-13-518 (Washington, D.C.: June 26, 2013).

[7] GAO, *Intragovernmental Revolving Funds: Commerce Departmental and Census Working Capital Funds Should Better Reflect Key Operating Principles*, GAO-12-56 (Washington, D.C.: Nov. 18, 2011). Also see GAO, *Air Force Working Capital Fund: Budgeting and Management of Carryover Work and Funding Could Be Improved*, GAO-11-539 (Washington, D.C.: July 7, 2011).

What Are the Sources and Fiscal Characteristics of the Funding?

The sources and fiscal characteristics of the funding influence what opportunities may exist for budgetary savings. Discretionary and mandatory funds present different issues in changing the size of any balance. Since discretionary accounts are controlled by the annual appropriations process, the size of any carryover balance can also be controlled through that process. Mandatory funding is budget authority provided in laws other than appropriations acts, such as authorizing acts. In such cases, to change or reduce the size of carryover balances, changes need to be made to authorizing language affecting program or eligibility requirements, for example. Moreover, since mandatory funds are often provided in "such sums as may be necessary" to make payments to those eligible, reducing the balance in such an account may have no practical or economic benefit and instead could impose unnecessary administrative costs. In other words, the action or effort to rescind a portion of mandatory balances would be countered by the action or effort to restore those funds because individuals are entitled to payments.

The time limits imposed upon the funds (period of availability for new obligation) are important to evaluating carryover balances. If an account receives multi-year or no-year appropriations, some accounts or programs should be expected to have carryover balances. Similarly, if an account receives multi-year supplemental appropriations late in the fiscal year or for long-term projects, there is an increased likelihood, and perhaps expectation, for a carryover balance in the account. Nevertheless, a growing carryover balance over a number of years may indicate challenges in executing a program as planned.

Accounts that receive funding primarily from outside sources, such as fees, have their own unique considerations. For example, an account that is fully funded through user fees that are available without further Congressional action may retain an unobligated balance to mitigate cyclical changes in fee revenue, thereby increasing assurance that sufficient funds will be available to support related mission activities. We are separately reporting on agencies' management of user fees and the identification and management of unobligated balances in fee-funded agencies.[8]

> **Examples of specific questions to understand how the sources and fiscal characteristics of the funding affect balances include**
>
> - Are the account or program funds mandatory, discretionary, or a combination of both?
>   - In accounts or programs that receive both mandatory and discretionary funds, what portion of each are unobligated each year?
> - What is the expected period over which funds will be obligated and liquidated (i.e., multiple years versus single year)?
>   - If multiple years, what drives the timing of the obligation and liquidation of funds (e.g., contract award period, grant cycle)?
> - Did the account receive supplemental appropriations?
>   - If so, when were the supplemental appropriations acts enacted? How much of the balance is attributed to supplemental appropriations?
> - To what extent is the activity funded by fees or dedicated taxes versus general revenues?
>   - Does the account or program have the authority to use the fees or taxes without additional congressional action?

What Factors Affect the Size or Composition of the Carryover Balance?

Some factors are within an agency's control and some are not. The rate at which obligations are incurred and subsequently liquidated in a fiscal year—that is, the rate at which budget authority becomes outlays—can vary with the nature of the activity. Understanding what drives this "spendout rate" provides information on the size of the unobligated portion of the balance versus the obligated portion; this in turn provides insight into the composition of the carryover balance as a whole. For example, for an account that funds procurement or grant activities, if the timing of the procurement cycle or grant award cycle differs from the fiscal year, the account is likely to have a slower spendout rate. As a result, the account may have a larger share of unobligated funds reported at the end of the fiscal year, which are then quickly obligated early in the following fiscal year. Alternatively, it could have a large obligated portion of the balance, which is expended over time.

---

[8] GAO, *Federal User Fees: A Design Guide*, GAO-08-386SP (Washington, D.C.: May 29, 2008). Also see *Federal User Fees: Fee Design Options and Implications for Managing Revenue Instability*, GAO-13-820 (Washington, D.C.: Sept. 30, 2013).

External events beyond agencies' control—such as natural disasters or economic crises—can dramatically affect carryover balances. For example, if an agency receives a sudden inflow of funds late in the fiscal year from an emergency supplemental appropriation, the size of the unobligated balance carried forward to the next fiscal year may be greater than otherwise estimated.

Examples of specific questions to understand what affects the size and composition of balances include

- How has the account's balance changed over time? How has the composition of the carryover balance (i.e., the unobligated and obligated portions) changed over time?
    - Has the agency's rate of obligation significantly slowed or increased as a result of certain factors (e.g., application or review periods, regulatory issuance)?
- What portion of unobligated funds has the agency labeled as committed for specific uses?
- What conditions or external events have occurred outside the agency's control (e.g., events that led to changes in program demand)?
    - Were there any changes to accounting, regulatory, or statutory requirements related to the account's balance (e.g., bid protests, receipt of supplemental appropriations, continuing resolutions)?
- Are there questions about the agency's ability or capacity to carry out the program due to previously reported weaknesses (e.g., excessive risks, poor performance, unmet objectives)?
- Are interim milestones being met to ensure projects are carried out on schedule?
    - Are there known production issues that could lead to delays?
- What opportunities exist to deobligate unliquidated balances (e.g., up-front obligations to contractors, grants to states)?

How Does the Agency Estimate and Manage Carryover Balances?

Understanding an agency's processes for estimating and managing carryover balances provides information to assess how effectively agencies anticipate program needs and ensure the most efficient use of resources. If an agency does not have a robust strategy in place to manage carryover balances, or is unable to adequately explain or support the reported carryover balance, then a more in-depth review is warranted. In those cases, balances may either fall too low to efficiently manage operations or rise to unnecessarily high levels, producing potential opportunities for those funds to be used more efficiently elsewhere.

> **Examples of specific questions to understand how agency estimation and management practices affect balances include**
>
> - What assumptions or factors did the agency incorporate into its estimate of the account's carryover balance (e.g., historical experience, demand models)?
> - To what extent and how often does the agency revisit or adjust estimates of unobligated balances to reflect historical data or other information?
> - Does the agency have a routine mechanism for reviewing its obligations and determining whether there are opportunities to deobligate funds (e.g., written procedures or ad hoc processes)?
> - What is the agency's timeline for obligating and expending funds in the account?
>   - Does the agency or program tend to under-execute its budget?
>   - What is the spendout rate after funds have been obligated?
> - Has the agency followed its own procedures for ensuring fiscally responsible management of balances?

Selected Agencies Managed Balances According to Mission, Funding, Operations, and Estimated Demand for Services

To provide context and perspective in terms of an individual account or program, we selected a nongeneralizable sample of eight accounts and conducted further analysis of their carryover balances (see table 2). Our analysis is framed in the context of the four key overarching questions presented in the previous section. For the purpose of this report, we did not seek to identify specific savings related to the selected accounts. Detailed information on our analysis of each of the eight accounts is presented in appendix III.

Table 2: Eight Selected Accounts for Further Review

Account name (department)	Designation
Government Sponsored Enterprise Preferred Stock Purchase Agreements (Dept. of the Treasury)	Mandatory
Exchange Stabilization Fund (Dept. of the Treasury)	Mandatory
Federal Housing Administration-Mutual Mortgage Insurance Capital Reserve (Dept. of Housing and Urban Development)	Mandatory
Community Development Fund (Dept. of Housing and Urban Development)	Split
U.S. Army Corps of Engineers Civil Works-Construction (Dept. of Defense)	Discretionary
Public Health and Social Services Emergency Fund (Dept. of Health and Human Services)	Discretionary
Army Aircraft Procurement (Dept. of Defense)	Discretionary
Homeless Assistance Grants (Dept. of Housing and Urban Development)	Discretionary

Source: GAO analysis of OMB MAX data.

Note: Split accounts contain both mandatory and discretionary funds.

Carryover Balances Supported Programmatic Mission

The accounts in our review contained carryover balances so that they could support the agency's ability to carry out its mission. The eight accounts we reviewed received multi-year or no-year funds and supported a wide variety of missions, such as homeless assistance, aquatic ecosystem restoration, disaster recovery, financial market stability, and military readiness. Accordingly, the specific types of activities funded through the accounts varied as well, including construction projects, procurement, grants, and emergency preparedness.[9] Over the fiscal year 2007 through 2012 period, each of the accounts had a carryover balance that was tied to the manner in which the agency went about fulfilling its related mission responsibilities.

For example, the Mutual Mortgage Insurance Capital Reserve account maintains a balance for unexpected insurance claim expenses and was established to hold reserve funds to meet Federal Housing Administration's (FHA) Mutual Mortgage Insurance Fund (MMI Fund) statutory capital reserve requirement. Under the MMI Fund, FHA insures a variety of mortgages for home purchases and refinancing to meet the housing needs of traditionally underserved borrowers.[10] The carryover balance in the capital reserve account is composed entirely of unobligated funds and is affected by changes in the anticipated performance of FHA-insured mortgages. Consequently, the housing crisis that started in 2007 had a significant effect on the size of the account's unobligated balance. During the housing crisis, the balance was drawn down as more pessimistic forecasts of economic conditions—house prices, in particular—resulted in higher projected insurance claims. In fiscal year 2007, the unobligated balance was approximately $21 billion, but the balance had decreased to $3.3 billion by fiscal year 2012.

Alternatively, the Government Sponsored Enterprise (GSE) Preferred Stock Purchase Agreements account was established to preserve liquidity in the housing market through two GSEs: (1) the Federal National Mortgage Association (Fannie Mae) and (2) the Federal Home Loan Mortgage Corporation (Freddie Mac). The account maintains a carryover balance composed entirely of unobligated funds, which is designed such

---

[9] An individual account may support an entire program, a portion of a program, or multiple programs.

[10] FHA also insures reverse mortgages that permit persons 62 and older to convert their home equity into cash advances.

that the Department of the Treasury (Treasury) has the authority to transfer sums as needed to the GSEs to ensure their positive net worth; that is, when the two GSEs' liabilities exceed assets. Such payments are made on a quarterly basis if needed and decrease the account balance accordingly. Created in 2008, the account's unobligated balance peaked in 2009 at $304 billion, after Congress authorized an increase to the allowable funding commitment Treasury could provide to the GSEs. Subsequently, the balance gradually declined through 2012.[11]

Sources and Fiscal Characteristics of Funding Affected Timing and Use of Balances

The sources of funding and their fiscal characteristics across our sample of accounts varied. Three accounts were made up of solely mandatory amounts, four consisted solely of discretionary funds, and one account was split: it had a combination of both mandatory and discretionary funds. Accounts in our review that received discretionary funds were funded by annual appropriations and supplemental appropriations. The period of availability of funds included multi-year and no-year money provided through annual or supplemental appropriations, or both.

The sources and fiscal characteristics of funding for an account or program affect the timing of when funds are obligated and disbursed, and provide insight into why amounts may be carried forward from one fiscal year to the next. For example, in some cases where an account received supplemental appropriations, the level of carryover funds was significantly affected by the timing of that supplemental appropriation. For example, the Community Development Fund (CDF) account, which primarily supports the Community Development Block Grant (CDBG) program, received a large supplemental appropriation on September 30, 2008, to provide disaster relief to areas affected by hurricanes, floods, and other natural disasters. The receipt of supplemental funds at the end of the fiscal year caused a significant spike in the account's carryover balance for that year.

Additionally, the timing of final appropriations decisions had a significant effect on the size of unobligated balances in certain accounts. When continuing resolutions (CR) are enacted in lieu of annual appropriations bills, it creates uncertainty about both the timing and level of funding that ultimately will be available. For example, agencies are directed to operate

---

[11] As part of the purchase agreements with the GSEs, Treasury was entitled to receive cumulative cash dividends on the senior preferred stock from the date of initial issuance through December 31, 2012. These amounts were deposited in the General Fund.

at a conservative rate of spending while CRs are in effect, thus compressing the time period to obligate funds once final appropriations decisions are made. We have previously reported that this also limits an agency's management options.[12] In addition to affecting the rate of obligations, agencies may be uncertain how Congress will ultimately choose to direct funds until final appropriations decisions are made. For example, the U.S. Army Corps of Engineers develops and presents construction plans for specific projects as part of its annual budget request. Corps officials reported that in some cases, committee reports accompanying appropriations acts included language directing the Corps to carry out additional construction projects than those which already had work plans developed. Consequently, Corps officials said obligating the funds to support these additional priorities was delayed while they developed the necessary work plans.

Agency Operations Affected the Size and Composition of Carryover Balances

For each of the accounts in our review, the way an agency or program operates affected the size and composition of carryover balances. During fiscal years 2007 through 2012, the size of the carryover balances in each of the eight accounts we reviewed ranged from a low of $2.5 billion in the U.S. Army Corps of Engineers-Civil Works Construction account to $304 billion in Treasury's GSE Preferred Stock Purchase Agreements account. Depending on the needs of the program and the way the agency managed the funding, the portion of the carryover balance attributed to unobligated versus obligated also varied across the eight accounts. For example, the GSE purchase agreement account, which was created in 2008, had a large unobligated balance and no obligated balance. The account made direct quarterly payments to Fannie Mae and Freddie Mac as needed. The spendout rate was very quick—that is, funds were disbursed soon after obligation—which resulted in the agency reporting no obligated balance in the account by year end. Accordingly, the remaining unobligated balance represents the cash balance in the account.

In contrast, the carryover balance in Army's Aircraft Procurement account was largely made up of unliquidated obligations. This was due, in part, to the nature of the procurement cycle, which results in a slower spendout rate. As the agency entered into a contract, funds were obligated up front

---

[12] GAO, *Continuing Resolutions: Uncertainty Limited Management Options and Increased Workload in Selected Agencies*, GAO-09-879 (Washington, D.C.: Sept. 24, 2009).

to reflect the government's liability. However, funds were disbursed only as work was completed according to the terms of the contract.

In the case of the grant accounts we reviewed, the size of the carryover balance depended on the particular grant cycle. For example, the carryover balance in the Department of Housing and Urban Development's (HUD) Homeless Assistance Grants account contained a relatively smaller portion of unobligated funds compared to obligated funds. The unobligated balance resulted from the timing of the grant award process, which is done on a calendar year rather than fiscal year basis. Consequently, while a portion of funds are unobligated at the end of the fiscal year, the agency plans to award grants at a later date during the current or next calendar year, likely during a new fiscal year, at which point the available multi-year funds will be obligated. The size of the obligated but unliquidated balance depends on the rate at which the grantees draw down, or spend, the funds.

Some accounts experienced a dramatic spike in their balances while others remained relatively steady. For example, when the Exchange Stabilization Fund (ESF) received almost $50 billion in allocations from the International Monetary Fund (IMF) over a one-month period late in fiscal year 2009, the unobligated balance spiked. Treasury officials said the new allocations were an important element of the response to the global economic crisis. In addition, beginning in fiscal year 2010, the size of the obligated portion of the balance in the account grew dramatically after Treasury implemented a budgetary reporting change that resulted in significant adjustments to ESF account balances for fiscal years 2010 through 2012.

Estimation and Management of Carryover Balances Differed between Mandatory and Discretionary Accounts

The methods by which agencies in our sample estimated future carryover balances depended, in part, on whether the account was mandatory or discretionary. In the case of mandatory accounts, agencies focused on future needs of the account and relied on economic indicators as well as historical trends to estimate future balances of the account, including carryover balances. For example, budget-year estimates of carryover balances in the GSE Preferred Stock Purchase Agreements account are derived from the projected draws—payments to the two GSEs—from year to year. To do this, Treasury annually prepares a series of long-range forecasts to determine the estimated amount of contingent liability to the GSEs under the purchase agreements. Based on the size of the projected payments, Treasury estimates the amount of budget authority that will be carried over into the next fiscal year.

Similarly, estimated future carryover balances for the Exchange Stabilization Fund (ESF) represent projected net interest earnings on investments. The estimates are subject to considerable variation, depending on changes in the amount and composition of assets and the interest rates applied to investments.

Among the eight accounts we reviewed, the discretionary accounts used historical data combined with current variables to estimate carryover balances. For example, when estimating the carryover amounts in HUD's Homeless Assistance Grants (HAG) account, officials said they look at the composition of the balance over recent years, including factors such as historical rates of obligations and outlays. Additionally, officials estimate balances based on experience of which programs are likely to request renewals. Estimating the use of the program based on historical trends helps officials estimate both the unobligated and obligated portion of carryover balances.

Concluding Observations

Given the fiscal pressures facing the nation, examination of carryover balances provides an opportunity for enhanced oversight of agencies' management of federal funds. It also may help identify areas where the federal government can improve and maximize the use of resources. The increase in the size of total end-of-year carryover balances across the federal government between fiscal years 2007 through 2012 may raise questions. Is the balance in an account or program appropriate? Does an account or program with a significant or growing balance need these funds? Do the balances indicate there are opportunities to reduce or rescind balances and direct those resources towards other programs or priorities?

There is no single answer to these questions—they depend on the characteristics of the specific account or program in question. The answer requires an analysis of the mission, funding, composition, and agency management of carryover balances. Understanding the mission activities and goals supported by the account or program in question enhances the ability of decision makers and reviewers to see the trade-offs or risks involved in deciding to reduce a carryover balance and the consequential effect on the agency's ability to achieve its mission. Understanding the details of the fiscal characteristics and source of funding for the account or program can highlight the boundaries where real savings opportunities exist versus those that would have no real economic benefit.

Careful examination can also provide information about changes in factors affecting budget execution in the relevant area. Not all factors affecting the size and composition of balances are within an agency's control. Nevertheless, taking into consideration the agency's processes for estimating carryover balances and its ability to effectively manage balances throughout the year can draw attention to good practices as well as areas where execution could be improved. Given the complex characteristics of the various accounts and programs that constitute the federal budget, the most effective way to identify real opportunities for savings from carryover balances is to analyze them on an account-by-account or program-by-program basis.

Agency Comments and Our Evaluation

We provided a draft of this report to the Secretaries of Defense, Health and Human Services, Housing and Urban Development, and the Treasury for review and comment. All four departments generally agreed with our findings and provided technical comments that were incorporated as appropriate. HHS provided comments that are discussed below and reprinted in appendix IV.

The comments submitted by the HHS Assistant Secretary for Legislation stressed the need to recognize that our audit focused on a select number of federal accounts, which may or may not be representative of all government accounts with carryover balances. Furthermore, HHS said that any conclusions drawn from the report may not apply across the board to all accounts with multi-year or no-year funds. As stated in multiple sections of our report, including the objectives, scope, and methodology section, we selected a nongeneralizable sample of eight accounts with multi-year or no-year funds to use as case illustrations to answer the four key overarching questions we identified in this report. Our draft report called attention to the varied and unique characteristics among the many accounts that make up the federal budget and the need to analyze balances on an account-by-account or program-by-program basis. Furthermore, we state that the list of evaluative questions we identified is not intended to represent all of the questions that could be considered when evaluating carryover balances.

HHS emphasized that the Public Health and Social Services Emergency Fund has complexities and authorities that may differ from other federal accounts. The agency stated that looking at trends over time in an account may not be the correct approach to overcome these complexities when trying to determine spend rates or reasons for fluctuations in spend rates. As noted above, multiple sections of the report cite the variety and uniqueness of the many accounts in the federal budget. Furthermore, as stated in the report, we deliberately chose a selection of accounts representing a variety of characteristics to give a sense of the range of issues that may be involved when evaluating carryover balances. We also emphasize that reviewing the carryover balance in an account for just a single year may reflect events particular to that year and so present an incomplete or possibly misleading view of what is happening in a given account or program. We still consider a longer view—that is, reviewing balances over multiple years—to be the more preferable approach.

We are sending copies of this report to the Secretaries of Defense, Health and Human Services, Housing and Urban Development, and the Treasury. We are also sending copies of this report to relevant congressional committees. In addition, the report is available at no charge on GAO's website at http://www.gao.gov.

If you or your staff have any questions about this report, please contact Susan J. Irving at (202) 512-6806 or irvings@gao.gov. Contact points for our Offices of Congressional Relations and Public Affairs may be found on the last page of this report. GAO staff who have made contributions to this report are listed in appendix VI.

Sincerely,

Susan J. Irving
Director for Federal Budget Analysis
Strategic Issues

Appendix I: Overview of Carryover Balances across Federal Accounts in Fiscal Years 2007 through 2012

The size of the overall carryover balances in the federal budget increased significantly from 2007 through 2012 with the unobligated portion representing approximately one-third of that total balance throughout the period. Specifically, the sum of total carryover balances across the federal government was $1.5 trillion in fiscal year 2007, of which $471 billion—approximately 30 percent—was unobligated. At the end of fiscal year 2012, the sum of total carryover balances across all accounts was $2.2 trillion, of which $788 billion—approximately 35 percent—was unobligated.[1]

The number of accounts with carryover balances also increased from fiscal years 2007 through 2012 with the majority of them reporting unobligated balances each year. Specifically, the number of accounts that reported carryover balances in fiscal year 2007 was 1,178, of which 895 reported unobligated balances, or approximately 76 percent. At the end of fiscal year 2012, the number of accounts that reported carryover balances was 1,274, of which nearly 1,000 reported unobligated balances, or approximately 78 percent.[2] Included in these numbers are some newly established accounts that were created by significant legislation during the federal government's response to the economic downturn and the housing crisis, such as the Housing and Economic Recovery Act of 2008, the Emergency Economic Stabilization Act of 2008,[3] and the 2009 American Recovery and Reinvestment Act.

The nature of the funds—whether they are mandatory, discretionary, or split[4]—influences what opportunities may exist for budgetary savings. For

---

[1] We analyzed the size, composition, and distribution of carryover balances across all accounts in the federal budget and how they changed during fiscal years 2007 through 2012. To do this, we collected and compared agencies' end-of-year actual unobligated balances plus their obligated balances for which payment had not yet been made. These data were queried from the Office of Management and Budget's (OMB) MAX database. To determine the reliability of the data, we cross-checked the MAX data against the numbers reported in the corresponding President's Budget Appendices. Data reported in MAX and the Budget Appendix are subject to rigorous review and checks through OMB to help ensure consistency of the data. Accordingly, such data were considered reliable for the purpose of this report.

[2] According to the President's Fiscal Year 2014 Budget Appendix, there were roughly 2,000 accounts that comprised the federal budget.

[3] Enactment of the Emergency Economic Stabilization Act authorized the establishment of the Troubled Asset Relief Program (TARP).

[4] Split accounts contain both mandatory and discretionary funds.

example, if the funds are primarily mandatory, programmatic changes are often necessary to change or reduce the size of carryover balances. Focusing only on the unobligated portion of carryover balances, figure 1 shows that mandatory accounts represented an increasing share of the federal government's unobligated balances.[5] Specifically, in fiscal year 2007, 23 percent of the total unobligated funds in federal accounts were attributed to mandatory accounts. By the end of fiscal year 2012, almost 48 percent of unobligated balances resided in mandatory accounts.

The 10 largest unobligated balances reported at the end of fiscal year 2012 were in accounts with mandatory or split funding (see table 3). The combined balances in those 10 accounts represented 58 percent of the total unobligated balances government-wide that year.

Table 3: Top Ten Largest Unobligated Balances, Fiscal Year 2012

Account name (department)	Designation	Amount (millions)
1. Government Sponsored Enterprise (GSE) Preferred Stock Purchase Agreements (Treasury)	Mandatory	$212,515
2. Exchange Stabilization Fund (Treasury)	Mandatory	44,092
3. Employees Life Insurance Fund (OPM)	Split	40,326
4. Deposit Insurance Fund (FDIC)	Split	37,455
5. Federal-aid Highways (Dept. of Transportation)	Split	30,018
6. U.S. Quota, International Monetary Fund (Treasury)	Mandatory	21,921
7. Grants to States for Medicaid (Dept. of Health and Human Services)	Mandatory	21,091
8. Employees and Retired Employees Health Benefits Fund (OPM)	Split	18,510
9. Pension Benefit Guaranty Corporation Fund (Dept. of Labor)	Split	15,582
10. Aircraft Procurement, Air Force (Dept. of Defense)	Split	14,876
Total		$456,386

Source: GAO analysis of OMB MAX data.

Note: Split accounts contain both mandatory and discretionary funds.

[5] Federal accounts are designated as mandatory, discretionary, or split. As defined earlier, mandatory refers to budget authority that is provided in laws other than appropriations acts. This includes funding for entitlement programs such as Medicare and veterans' pension programs. Discretionary refers to budget authority that is provided in and controlled by annual appropriations acts. Split accounts include both mandatory and discretionary funds.

As shown in figures that follow, during fiscal years 2007 through 2012, unobligated balances were concentrated in mandatory accounts and centered on three national priorities and eight agencies. The GSE Preferred Stock Purchase Agreements account, which was created in 2008,[6] held by far the largest unobligated balance and affected the composition of balances across the federal government accordingly.

Figure 2: Mandatory Accounts Represented an Increasing Share of Unobligated Balances, Fiscal Years 2007-2012

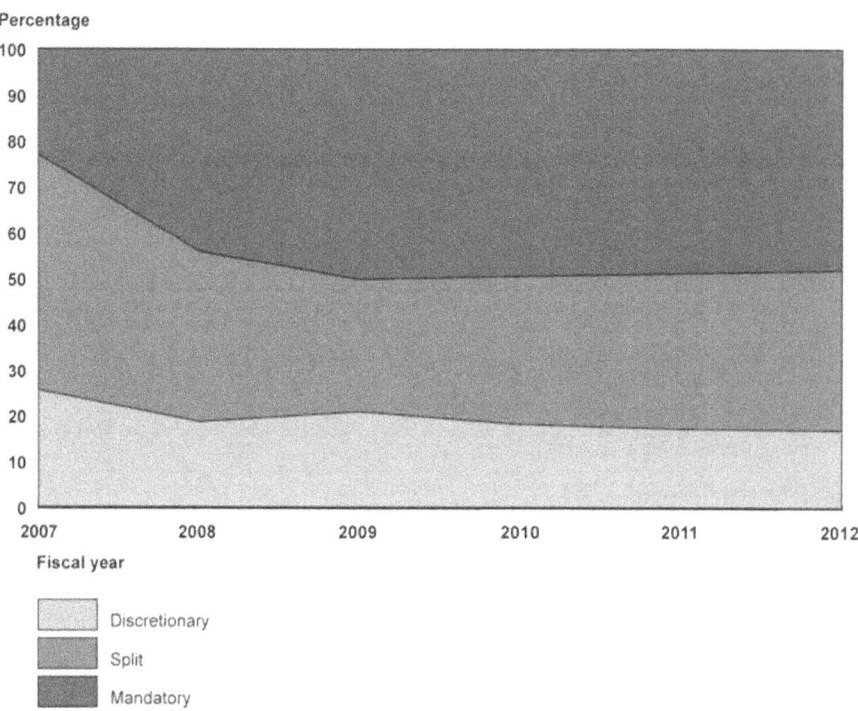

Percentage

Fiscal year

Discretionary

Split

Mandatory

Source: GAO analysis of OMB MAX data.

Note: Split accounts contain both mandatory and discretionary funds. During this period there were 14 additional accounts with reported unobligated balances. We do not include them here because the sum of the balances in those 14 accounts represented less than 0.01 percent of the total unobligated balances government-wide.

[6] Enactment of the Housing and Economic Recovery Act (HERA) placed two GSEs—(1) the Federal National Mortgage Association (Fannie Mae) and (2) the Federal Home Loan Mortgage Corporation (Freddie Mac)—into conservatorship and authorized the Department of Treasury to provide necessary funding to maintain liquidity.

The three largest mandatory accounts on average were Treasury's

- GSE Preferred Stock Purchase Agreement account,
- Exchange Stabilization Fund, and
- Troubled Asset Relief Program (TARP) Housing Programs.

Split accounts with both mandatory and discretionary funds made up roughly half of the unobligated balances government-wide in fiscal year 2007, but decreased to one-third by fiscal year 2012. The three largest split accounts on average were the

- Office of Personnel Management's Employee Life Insurance Fund,
- Federal Deposit Insurance Corporation's (FDIC) Deposit Insurance Fund, and
- Department of Transportation's (DOT) Federal-aid Highways account.

Discretionary accounts made up the smallest portion of unobligated balances across the federal budget. The three largest discretionary accounts on average were the

- Department of Education's State Fiscal Stabilization Fund established under the American Recovery and Reinvestment Act,
- Department of Defense's (DOD) Navy Shipbuilding and Conversion account, and
- DOT's Capital Assistance for High Speed Rail Corridors and Intercity Rail Service, established under the American Recovery and Reinvestment Act.

Each federal account is assigned to a budget function, which identifies the national priority supported by the account.[7] As shown in figure 3, the majority of unobligated balances were attributed to three national priorities: commerce and housing credit (function 370), national defense (function 050), and international affairs (function 150). In general throughout this period, commerce and housing credit accounted for the largest share of unobligated balances government-wide, growing from 21 percent in fiscal year 2007 to 37 percent at the end of fiscal year 2012.

---

[7] Budget function is a classification according to national priority or major purpose served (e.g. agriculture, transportation, income security). Each federal activity is placed into a single functional classification that best defines the activity's most important purpose, even though many activities serve more than one purpose. Major functions are further divided into subfunctions.

Three accounts contributed significantly to the share of unobligated balances attributed to commerce and housing credit: the GSE Preferred Stock Purchase Agreements account (newly created in fiscal year 2008), the Deposit Insurance Fund account, and the MMI Capital Reserve account.

Figure 3: Three National Priorities Accounted for the Largest Share of Unobligated Balances, Fiscal Years 2007-2012

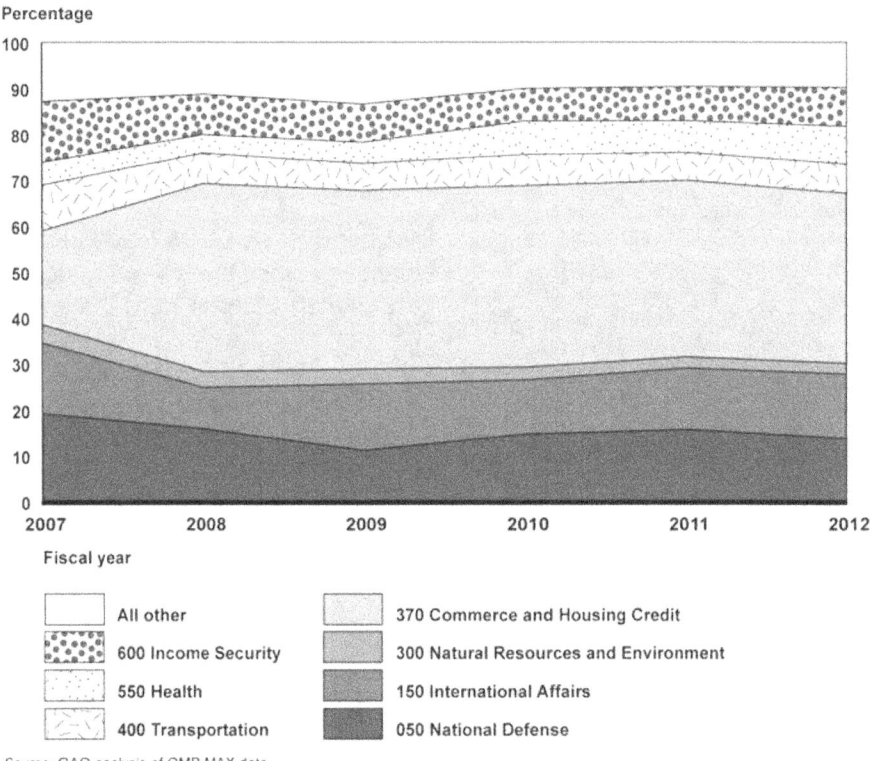

Percentage

Fiscal year

All other	370 Commerce and Housing Credit
600 Income Security	300 Natural Resources and Environment
550 Health	150 International Affairs
400 Transportation	050 National Defense

Source: GAO analysis of OMB MAX data.

Note: "All other" is composed of 12 other budget functions. Budget functions are coded with a three-digit number that directly correlates to a specific national priority.

The economic downturn and housing crisis and the government's response to it was also a major determinant of which agencies accounted for the majority of unobligated balances in fiscal years 2007 through 2012. As shown in figure 4, the share of unobligated balances held by Treasury, which manages the GSE Preferred Stock Purchase Agreement account, grew from 8 percent in fiscal year 2007 to 33 percent in fiscal year 2012. For most of the period, Treasury held the largest share of unobligated balances. DOD held the second largest share of unobligated balances over the period. Together these two (plus six other agencies that accounted for considerably smaller shares) represented approximately 80 percent of unobligated balances throughout the period. If the GSE Preferred Stock Purchase Agreement account was excluded from the breakdown shown in figure 4, DOD would represent the largest share of unobligated balances during the period.

Figure 4: Unobligated Balances Were Concentrated around Eight Agencies, Fiscal Years 2007-2012

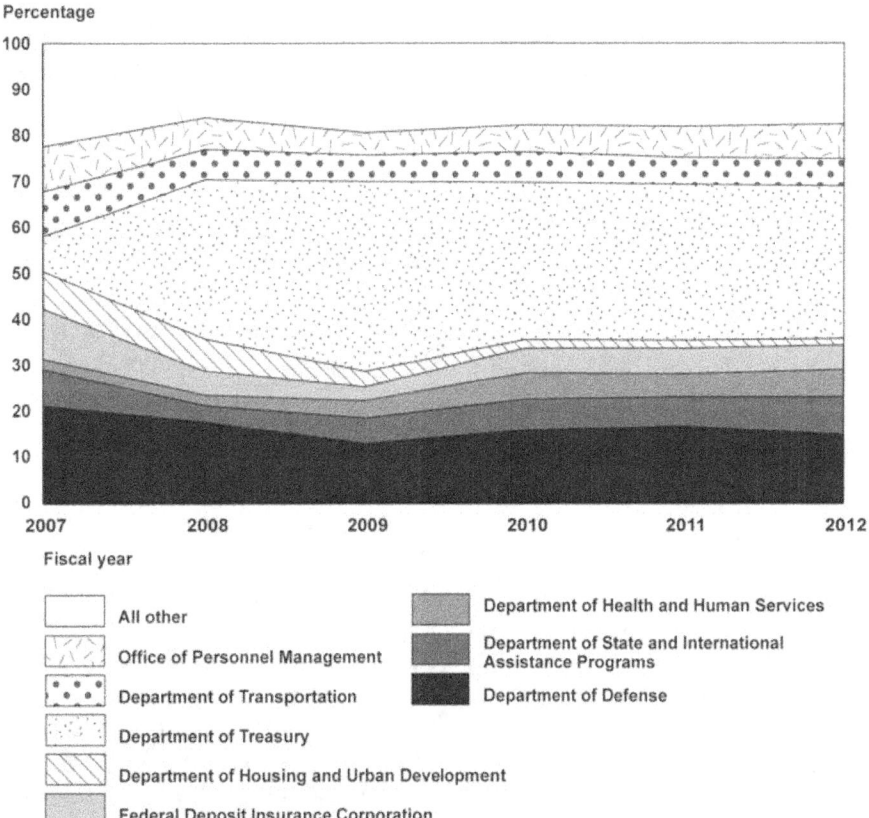

Source: GAO analysis of OMB MAX data.

Note: "All other" is composed of more than 100 departments/agencies such as the Department of Homeland Security and Social Security Administration. The Department of State and International Assistance Programs category includes other entities such as the U.S. Agency for International Development, the Millennium Challenge Corporation, and the Peace Corps.

Appendix II: Guide for Evaluating Carryover Balances

We developed four key overarching questions to consider in evaluating both obligated and unobligated balances. Each of these leads to a set of second-tier, more specific questions to help frame the analysis of carryover balances. We developed this list of questions from our analysis of government-wide guidance on budget preparation, budget execution, and internal controls. In addition, we met with federal budget specialists, agency officials responsible for managing the eight accounts selected as part of our review, and staff within the Office of Management and Budget (OMB) to obtain their views on the use of these questions to guide the examination of carryover balances. Our prior work on federal budgeting, user fees, budget triggers, and managing under continuing resolutions also informed the development of these key questions.

Answering each of the four overarching questions provides insight into why the balance exists, what size balance is appropriate, and what opportunities, if any, for savings exist. In addition, it may provide opportunities for enhanced oversight of agencies' management of federal funds and identify areas where the federal government can improve and maximize its use of resources. These questions can be applied when evaluating carryover balances at either the account or program level. A single account may support a single program or multiple programs. Conversely a single program may be supported by multiple accounts. Further, the balance in a single year may reflect events particular to that year and so present an incomplete or possibly misleading view of what is happening in a given account or program. Therefore, a longer view is preferable.

Since the many accounts that make up the federal budget vary greatly and individual accounts have their own unique characteristics, we do not suggest that the following set of questions represents all the questions that could be considered when evaluating carryover balances. As congressional committees, managers, and other reviewers apply these evaluative questions, additional questions may arise. In some cases, however, a few of the questions may provide sufficient information to understand the nature of the balance.

Key question	Subset of questions
What mission and goals is the account or program supporting? Understanding the mission activities, goals, and programs the account supports provides insight into whether a program needs to maintain a balance to operate smoothly, what size balance is appropriate, and whether opportunities for savings exist. Such context can inform assessments of whether and how to reduce carryover balances, and what effect this would have on the agency's ability to carry out its mission. For example, an account established to provide stability in the financial or housing market needs a balance to ensure the agency has sufficient resources to respond quickly to adverse events.	What are the primary mission and goals the account or program is intended to achieve?
	What is the nature and purpose of the balance and how does it support the mission and goals (e.g., counter economic crises, sustain business-like activities, meet emergency funding needs)?
	Have there been changes to the program or mission that may affect balances (e.g., additional responsibilities, major reorganization)?
	What type of activity (e.g., grants, procurement, direct services) is the account used for to achieve the agency's mission and goals? What are the implications of carryover balances?
	What programs are funded by the account and how much does each contribute, if at all, to the carryover balance (e.g., does a large portion of the balance result from any particular programs)?
	Is it a new account or program or have the program goals and objectives changed? • How has this affected the ability to obligate funds?
What are the sources and fiscal characteristics of the funding? The sources and fiscal characteristics of the funds influence what opportunities may exist for savings. If funds are primarily mandatory, opportunities are more limited as programmatic changes would generally be required to reduce balances. In such cases, reducing an account's balance may have no economic benefit and instead could impose unnecessary administrative costs. If funds are discretionary, balances can be controlled by the annual appropriations process. Some accounts or programs may be expected to have carryover balances if the agency has multi-year or no-year funds. Supplemental appropriations enacted late in the fiscal year (or for long-term projects) may also increase the likelihood, and perhaps expectation, for a carryover balance. However, a growing carryover balance over a number of years may indicate problems executing a program as planned. Accounts that receive funding primarily from outside sources, such as fees, have their own unique considerations.[1]	Are the account or program funds mandatory, discretionary or a combination of both? • In accounts or programs that receive both mandatory and discretionary funds, what portion of each are unobligated each year?
	For unobligated funds, what is the expected period over which funds will be obligated and liquidated (i.e., multiple years versus single year)? • If over multiple years, what drives the timing of the obligation and liquidation of funds (e.g., contract award period, grant cycle)?
	Did the account receive supplemental appropriations? • If so, when were the supplemental appropriations acts enacted? How much of the balance is attributed to supplemental appropriations?
	To what extent is the activity funded by fees or taxes (e.g., fuel taxes) versus general revenues? • Does the account or program have the authority to use the fees or taxes without additional congressional action?

---

[1] If fees are the primary source of funding, see questions to consider in GAO, *Federal User Fees: Fee Design Options and Implications for Managing Revenue Instability*, GAO-13-820 (Washington, D.C.: Sept. 30, 2013).

Key question	Subset of questions
What factors affect the size or composition of the carryover balance? It is important to consider which factors were within the agency's control and which were not. Agencies or programs may operate in a way that contributes to a faster or slower spendout rate for a particular account. Understanding the spendout rate can help to identify what drives the size of the unobligated and obligated portions of the balance. In addition, external events beyond agencies' control—such as natural disasters or economic crises—can dramatically affect carryover balances. For example, if an agency receives a sudden inflow of funds late in the fiscal year from a supplemental appropriation, the size of the unobligated balance carried forward to the next fiscal year may be greater than otherwise estimated.	How has the account's balance changed over time? How has the composition of the carryover balance (i.e., the unobligated and obligated portions) changed over time? • Has the agency's rate of obligation significantly slowed or increased as a result of certain factors (e.g., application or review periods, regulatory issuance)?
	What portion of unobligated funds has the agency labeled as committed for specific uses?
	What conditions or external events have occurred outside the agency's control (e.g., events that led to changes in program demand)? • Were there any changes to accounting, regulatory, or statutory requirements related to the account's balance (e.g., bid protests, receipt of supplemental appropriations, continuing resolutions)?
	Are there questions about the agency's ability or capacity to carry out the program due to previously reported weaknesses (e.g., excessive risks, poor performance, unmet objectives)?
	Are interim milestones being met to ensure projects are carried out on schedule? • Are there known production issues that could lead to delays?
	What opportunities exist to deobligate unliquidated balances (e.g., up-front obligations to contractors, grants to states)?
How does the agency estimate and manage carryover balances? Understanding an agency's processes for estimating and managing carryover balances provides information to assess how effective agencies are in anticipating program needs and ensuring the most efficient use of resources. If an agency does not have a robust strategy in place to manage carryover balances or is unable to adequately explain or support the reported carryover balance, then a more in-depth review is warranted with the potential to identify opportunities for budgetary savings.	What assumptions or factors did the agency incorporate into its estimate of the account's carryover balance (e.g., historical experience, demand models)?
	To what extent and how often does the agency revisit or adjust estimates of unobligated balances to reflect historical data or other information?
	Does the agency have a routine mechanism for reviewing its obligations and determining whether there are opportunities to deobligate funds (e.g., written procedures or ad hoc processes)?
	What is the agency's timeline for obligating and expending funds in the account? • Does the agency or program tend to under-execute its budget? • What is the spendout rate after funds have been obligated?
	Has the agency followed its own procedures for ensuring fiscally responsible management of balances?

Source: GAO analysis.

Appendix III: Case Illustrations of Federal Accounts with Carryover Balances

As part of our review, we selected a nongeneralizable sample of eight accounts and analyzed their end-of-year carryover balances for fiscal years 2007 through 2012. These eight accounts serve as case illustrations to better understand why carryover balances existed and the types of factors that affected the size of the balances. We selected accounts based on several characteristics including the size of the average unobligated balance, budget function, type of account, agency, and whether the account was composed of mandatory or discretionary funds.

Our analysis is presented in terms of the four overarching key questions we developed in our evaluative guide outlined in appendix II. Because of the variation in the size of the accounts, the graphics depicted in each case illustration are scaled to the size of the individual account; as a result, the graphics cannot be directly compared to one another. Further, the second figure in each case illustration includes both actual unobligated balances as well as two sets of estimates: budget year and current year. The budget year (BY) is a term used in the budget formulation process to refer to the fiscal year for which the budget is being considered. For example, estimates for the fiscal year 2012 budget year were reported during fiscal year 2011. Current year (CY) is a term used in the budget formulation process to refer to the fiscal year immediately preceding the budget year under consideration; such that for fiscal year 2012, current year estimates were reported part way through 2012.

The eight accounts we reviewed as case illustrations were:

- Department of Defense: Army Aircraft Procurement
- Department of Defense: U.S. Army Corps of Engineers-Civil Works, Construction
- Department of Health and Human Services: Public Health and Social Services Emergency Fund
- Department of Housing and Urban Development: Community Development Fund
- Department of Housing and Urban Development: Federal Housing Administration-Mutual Mortgage Insurance Capital Reserve
- Department of Housing and Urban Development: Homeless Assistance Grants
- Department of the Treasury: Exchange Stabilization Fund
- Department of the Treasury: Government Sponsored Enterprise (GSE) Preferred Stock Purchase Agreements

Account Name:	Aircraft Procurement, Army (APA)
Agency:	Department of Defense
National Priority:	Department of Defense-Military
	(Budget Subfunction 051)

What Mission and Goals Is the Account or Program Supporting?

The Army uses the Aircraft Procurement account for construction, procurement, production, modification, and modernization of aircraft equipment. The Army purchases and maintains aircraft in order to support activities such as combat missions and operations. For example, the Army has a contract to develop an unmanned aircraft system, which will be able to carry four aircraft as well as other necessary equipment.

What Are the Sources and Fiscal Characteristics of the Funding?

APA receives annual and supplemental appropriations that are available for obligation for three years. All funds in the account are discretionary.

What Factors Affect the Size or Composition of the Carryover Balance?

As shown in figure 5, carryover balances increased steadily from approximately $7 billion in fiscal year 2007 to $13 billion in fiscal year 2011 before then decreasing slightly at the end of fiscal year 2012. The majority of the carryover balance was composed of unliquidated obligations.

Figure 5: Carryover Balances in the Army's Aircraft Procurement Account, Fiscal
Years 2007-2012

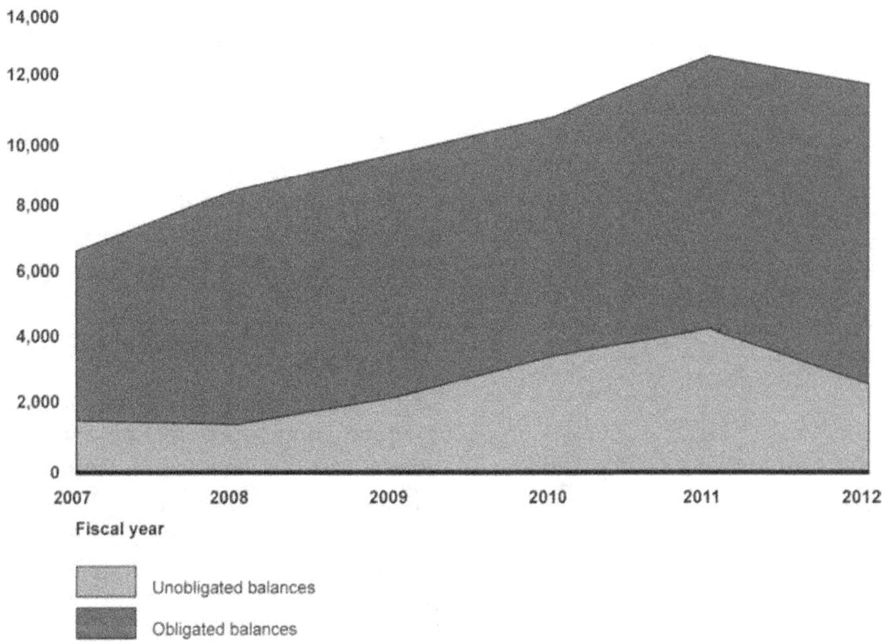

Source: GAO analysis of OMB MAX data.

Note: Balances shown here are end-of-year.

According to DOD officials, the majority of the carryover balance is
obligated but unliquidated due to the nature of the procurement process
for aircraft, which can take many years. Once the Army identifies a
requirement and receives appropriations to fund that requirement, it
issues a request for proposals to develop a product to meet the
requirement. After the request for proposal is issued, awarding a contract
generally takes three to nine months. Once a contract is in place and
funds are obligated, the agency periodically disburses funds to the
contractor as milestones are reached. The majority of the payment is
made upon delivery.

DOD officials said a portion of unobligated funds are committed
(reserved) for specific projects. However, balances that are considered
"committed" are not officially obligated until a contract is awarded. For
example, in 2011 the subaccount dedicated to modifications of aircraft
had an unobligated balance of about $420,000, of which approximately

$355,000, or about 85 percent, was already "committed" to specific projects.

In 2009, several events contributed to a delay in the contracting cycle that resulted in higher unobligated balances for 2010 and 2011. A 2009 executive policy memo directed DOD to issue new guidance regarding sole-source contracting. In anticipation of the guidance, APA officials chose to wait to award any further contracts. Additionally that year, we identified issues with the Defense Contract Audit Agency, including with the independence of their auditors.[1] As a result of these two factors, APA reviewed and revised its processes, which delayed the contracting timeline that year from approximately 3 to 9 months to 9 to 18 months.

How Does the Agency Estimate and Manage Carryover Balances?

DOD estimates carryover balances for the Army Aircraft Procurement account using a formula based on historical data. The agency first determines the average obligation rate over the previous five years. Using this weighted average, officials then apply that rate against current obligated balances in the account to estimate the amount of unobligated funds and unliquidated obligations that will carry forward to the next fiscal year.

As shown in figure 6, actual unobligated balances have steadily risen, while estimates have remained fairly steady. Further, actual unobligated balances were higher than estimates for all years, with the greatest differences occurring in 2010 through 2012. This suggests that the agency's model for estimating unobligated balances was fairly accurate for 2007 and 2008, and generally underestimated unobligated balances for years 2009 through 2012.

[1] GAO, *DCAA Audits: Widespread Problems with Audit Quality Require Significant Reform.* GAO-09-468 (Washington, D.C.: Sept. 23, 2009).

Figure 6: Estimated vs. Actual Unobligated Balances in the Army's Aircraft
Procurement Account, Fiscal Years 2007-2012

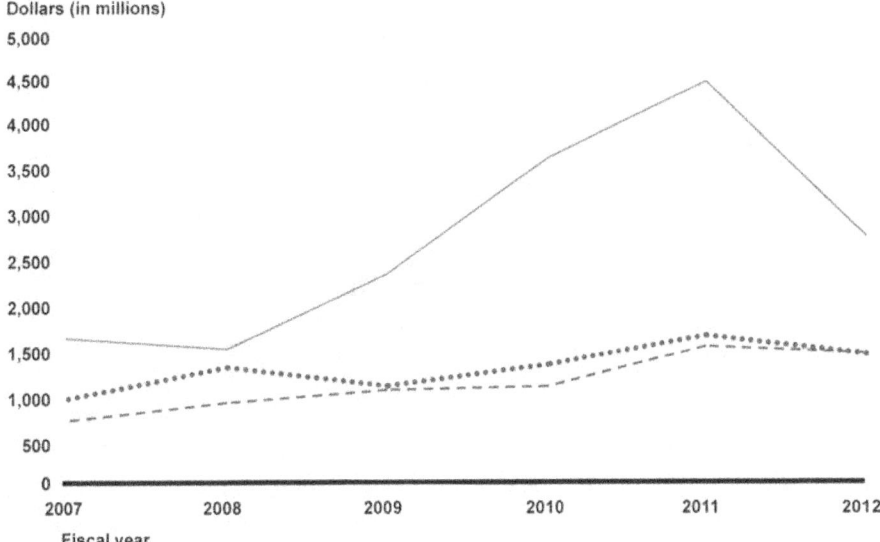

Source: GAO analysis of OMB data.

Note: Balances shown here are end-of-year.

Account Name:	Construction
Agency:	U.S. Army Corps of Engineers-Civil Works
National Priority:	Water Resources (Budget Subfunction 301)

What Mission and Goals Is the Account or Program Supporting?

The U.S. Army Corps of Engineers' (Corps) Construction account funds three main mission areas: flood and storm damage reduction, commercial navigation, and aquatic ecosystem restoration within the United States. The Corps engages in projects in waterways throughout the nation, such as in Ohio, Pennsylvania, Illinois, and Kentucky. While some projects are short term, others are long term and may involve a series of steps, such as rehabilitating a dam over time. The account allocates funding by project based on Congressional direction generally provided in committee reports accompanying the Corps' appropriations, as well as various performance-based guidelines, including projects with very high economic and environmental returns and those close to completion.

What Are the Sources and Fiscal Characteristics of the Funding?

The Construction account receives funding through both annual and supplemental appropriations. Annual appropriations are allocated by projects. All funds in the account are discretionary and are typically available until expended. In addition, the account receives transfers from other sources including the Inland Waterways Trust Fund and the Harbor Maintenance Trust Fund. The account also receives funds from other federal agencies including the Department of Homeland Security and the Department of Veterans' Affairs for specific construction projects.

What Factors Affect the Size or Composition of the Carryover Balance?

As shown in figure 7, during fiscal years 2007 through 2012 carryover balances peaked at nearly $10 billion in fiscal year 2009 before gradually decreasing to $5 billion in fiscal year 2012. The majority of the carryover balance was unobligated funds.

Figure 7: Carryover Balances in U.S. Army Corps of Engineers-Civil Works
Construction Account, Fiscal Years 2007-2012

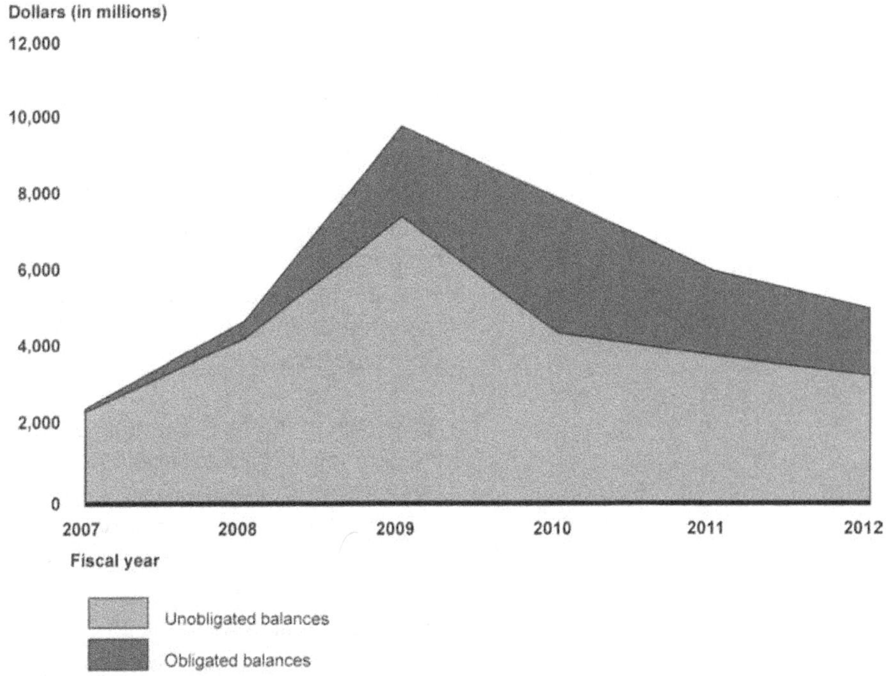

Source: GAO analysis of OMB MAX data.

Note: Balances shown here are end-of-year.

A portion of the carryover balance is a result of no-year supplemental
appropriations. Corps officials said that, in some cases, supplemental
funds were not intended to be obligated immediately because they fund
long-term projects. For example, between fiscal years 2006 and 2009, the
Construction account received approximately $5 billion to aid in disaster
recovery following Hurricane Katrina, a portion of which had still not been
expended in 2012. In fiscal years 2009 through 2012, the size of the
obligated portion of the balance was larger than in previous years as the
Corps had the opportunity to obligate funds from supplemental
appropriations it received.

Further, officials cited delays in final appropriations execution decisions
as a contributing factor to increased unobligated balances at the end of
each fiscal year. The Corps develops and presents construction plans for
specific projects as part of its annual budget request. In some cases,
committee reports accompanying appropriations acts included language

directing the Corps to carry out additional construction work beyond that for which the agency had already developed work plans. Consequently, Corps officials said obligating the funds to support this additional work was delayed until they developed the necessary work plans.

How Does the Agency Estimate and Manage Carryover Balances?

Corps officials said that carryover on individual projects is influenced by factors such as real estate and environmental considerations, including whether a project will affect local water quality. Officials also use ten-year historical averages of the account's obligations and outlays to identify possible trends that may affect balances going forward. To manage carryover balances, officials said they adjust work plans consistent with Congressional direction.

As shown in figure 8, the actual unobligated balance was larger than what the agency initially estimated each year during fiscal years 2007 through 2012. While in some cases, current year estimates were closer to actuals, the graph of estimated balances below suggests that the agency's estimation process generally underestimated the amount of unobligated funds that would be carried over each year. Agency officials said that in some cases, this was due to supplemental appropriations that were received after budget estimates were reported.

Figure 8: Estimated vs. Actual Unobligated Balances in the U.S. Army Corps of Engineers-Civil Works Construction Account, Fiscal Years 2007-2012

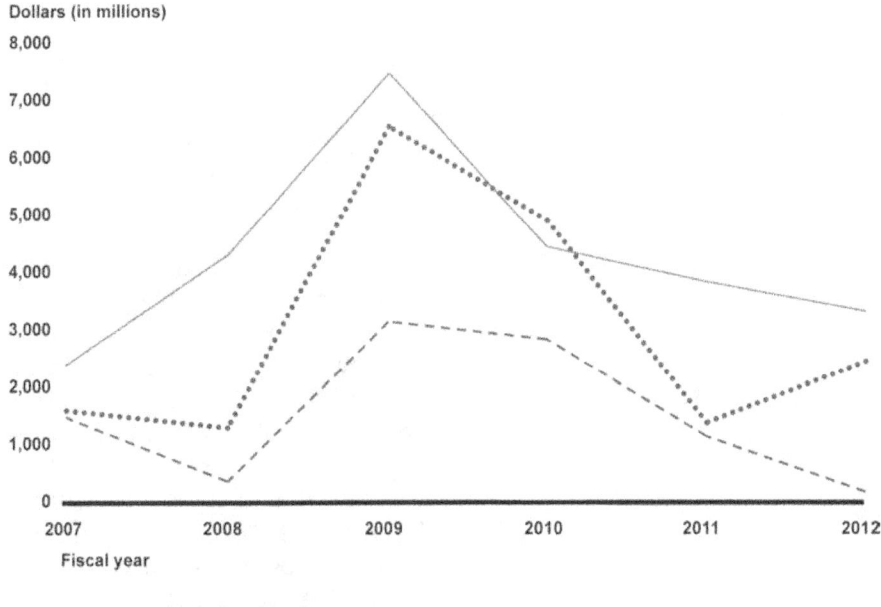

Source: GAO analysis of OMB data.

Note: Balances shown here are end-of-year.

Account Name: Public Health and Social Services
Emergency Fund (PHSSEF)
Agency: Department of Health and Human Services
National Priority: Health Care Services (Budget Subfunction 551)

What Mission and Goals Is the Account or Program Supporting?

The Department of Health and Human Services' (HHS) Public Health and
Social Services Emergency Fund (PHSSEF) provides resources to
support a comprehensive program to prepare for the public health and
medical consequences of bioterrorism or other public health
emergencies. Funds in this account support several offices and programs
tasked with emergency preparedness including the Office of the Assistant
Secretary for Preparedness and Response (ASPR), which receives the
largest share of appropriations in the account. Within ASPR, the largest
programs are the Hospital Preparedness Program and the Biomedical
Advanced Research and Development Authority. Other programs and
offices that PHSSEF supports include HHS' Cybersecurity program, the
Medical Reserve Corps, and Pandemic Influenza. In addition, the account
includes the balance of the Special Reserve Fund, which supports the
procurement of biodefense countermeasures as part of the Project
BioShield Act.[2]

What Are the Sources and Fiscal Characteristics of the Funding?

The account receives annual appropriations, supplemental
appropriations, and transfers from other accounts outside of HHS. Annual
appropriations primarily support ASPR and consist of a mix of both one-
year and multi-year funds. Supplemental appropriations were provided for

---

[2] In 2004, Congress passed the Project BioShield Act (Pub. L. No. 108-276) to provide the
federal government with new authorities related to the development, procurement, and
use of medical countermeasures against chemical, biological, radiological, and nuclear
(CBRN) terrorism agents. The act has three main provisions: (1) the creation of a
government-market guarantee by permitting the HHS Secretary to obligate funds to
purchase countermeasures while they still need several more years of development, (2)
the establishment of a process through which the HHS Secretary may temporarily allow
the emergency use of countermeasures that lack Food and Drug Administration (FDA)
approval, and (3) the provision of expedited procedures for HHS to spend CBRN
terrorism-related funds, including procuring products, hiring experts, and awarding
research grants. The balance in the Special Reserve Fund from fiscal year 2004
appropriations will no longer be available for obligation after September 30, 2013.

preparedness and response to pandemic influenza in 2009 and
emergency relief and reconstruction aid related to the earthquake in Haiti
in 2010. Those funds are available until expended (no-year funds). In
addition, the account received a transfer of funds from the Department of
Homeland Security for Project BioShield activities and reimbursements
from the Federal Emergency Management Agency. All funds in the
account are discretionary.

What Factors Affect the Size or Composition of Carryover Balances?

As shown in figure 9, the actual carryover balance dramatically increased
in fiscal year 2009, to approximately $11 billion, and subsequently
declined through 2012. In most years, the obligated portion of the balance
was greater than the unobligated portion. However, in fiscal year 2010,
with the receipt of supplemental appropriations, the unobligated balance
was almost twice as large as the obligated portion of the balance.

Figure 9: Carryover Balances in the Public Health and Social Services Emergency Fund, Fiscal Years 2007-2012

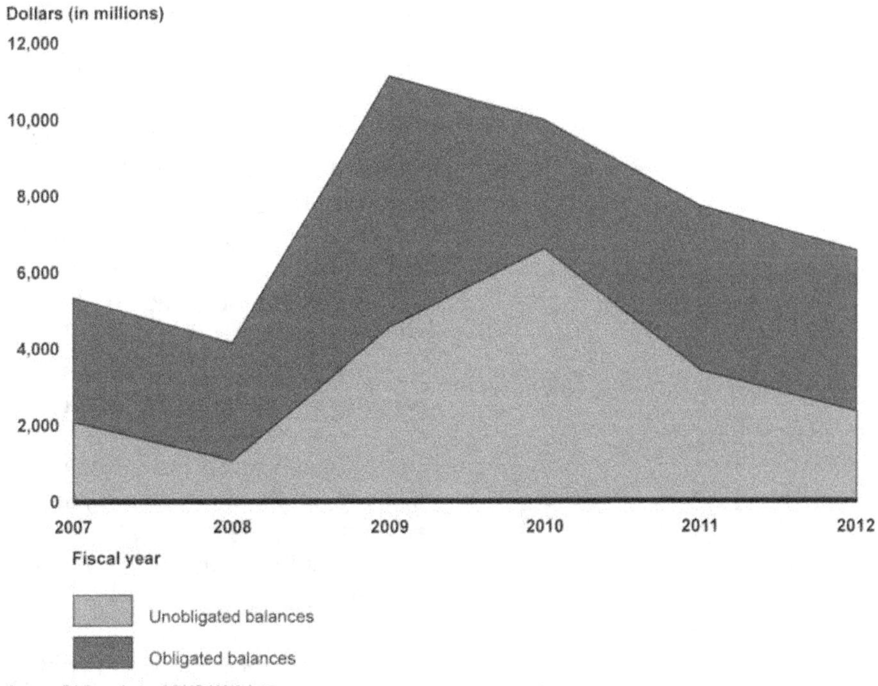

Source: GAO analysis of OMB MAX data.

Note: Balances shown here are end-of-year.

Agency officials said that carryover balances in the account were primarily the result of no-year supplemental appropriations. For example, in fiscal years 2009 and 2010, balances reflect supplemental appropriations to address the H1N1 pandemic influenza outbreak and emergency relief after the 2010 earthquake in Haiti. In addition, funds transferred from DHS for Project BioShield activities contributed to the carryover balance.

In addition, some of the multiple programs that PHSSEF supports have slower spendout rates than others. For example, agency officials explained that funds supporting Project BioShield activities were available for obligation at intervals over a ten-year period during fiscal years 2004 to 2013. They said the intent of the funding method was to provide procurement funds with availability over a long period of time to encourage industry to engage in the advanced development of countermeasures. As a result, some portion of unobligated funds would be carried forward each year. Once HHS has entered into a contract for the procurement of a specific countermeasure, agency officials said it may take years to progress through contractual milestones, thereby contributing to the size of the obligated portion of the carryover balance in any given year.

In contrast, agency officials said the spendout rate of PHSSEF funds supporting National Special Security Events (NSSE) is relatively shorter. Planned events which require HHS support include the Presidential Inauguration and July 4th celebrations on the National Mall. An example of an unplanned event is when HHS used PHSSEF funds to provide mental health response teams to Sandy Hook Elementary students, families, and staff after the school shooting in December 2012. HHS officials said the obligation of these funds for NSSE purposes is somewhat sporadic, but once obligated, funds are quickly disbursed.

How Does the Agency Estimate and Manage Carryover Balances?

Agency officials said the Office of Budget works with program and budget offices to obtain information to incorporate into budget year estimates of carryover balances. These balances are informed by prior year actuals and take into account any planned procurement, other contract actions, and grant awards.

As shown in figure 10, during fiscal years 2007 through 2012, actual unobligated balances in the account were higher than budget-year estimates in most years with the largest differences occurring in fiscal years 2009 and 2010. Agency officials said emergency supplemental appropriations contributed to higher than expected unobligated balances in 2009 and 2010. Specifically, supplemental appropriations were provided to address the influenza pandemic in 2009 and to respond to the earthquake in Haiti in 2010. Both events were unexpected and accordingly, were not included in the agency's initial estimates of the unobligated balance. In addition, HHS officials said obligations slowed in fiscal year 2010 when the influenza pandemic proved to be less severe than originally anticipated. In both 2011 and 2012 unobligated balances were lower than budget-year estimates.

Figure 10: Estimated vs. Actual Unobligated Balances in the Public Health and Social Services Emergency Fund, Fiscal Years 2007-2012

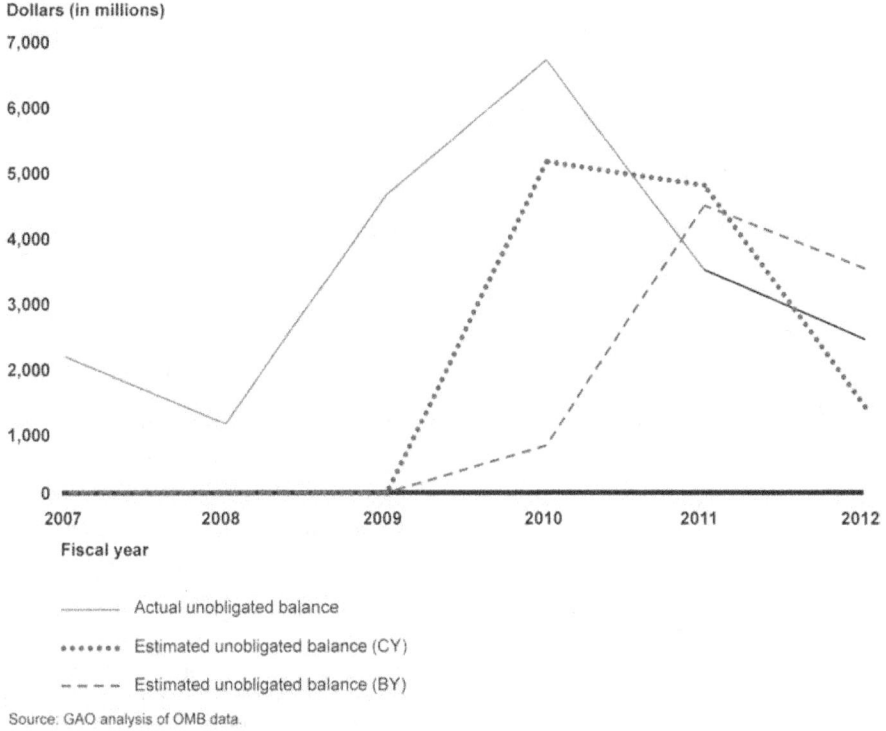

Source: GAO analysis of OMB data.

Note: Balances shown here are end-of-year.

Account Name: Community Development Fund (CDF)
Agency: Department of Housing and Urban Development
National Priority: Community Development
(Budget Subunction 451)

What Mission and Goals Is the Account or Program Supporting?

The Community Development Fund (CDF) primarily supports programs
targeted for low to moderate income individuals and families that include
activities such as job creation. The Department of Housing and Urban
Development (HUD) uses the funds in this account to distribute grant
assistance through several programs, the largest of which is the
Community Development Block Grant (CDBG). CDBG provides formula
grants to units of general local government and states to support activities
such as public infrastructure improvements, housing, rehabilitation, and
public service activities including child care.

CDF also supports other programs such as Section 108 loan
guarantees,[3] the Neighborhood Stabilization Program (NSP)[4] and
disaster recovery programs. CDF has received large supplemental
appropriations for various disaster recovery efforts such as those
following Hurricane Katrina and Hurricane Wilma.

What Are the Sources and Fiscal Characteristics of the Funding?

CDF receives annual CDBG appropriations for grants to state and local
governments which are available for obligation for three years. HUD
officials said that CDBG funds are distributed through formulas, with
approximately 70 percent allocated to entitlement communities and 30
percent to non-entitlement communities. According to HUD, entitlement

---

[3] The Section 108 Loan Guarantee Program provides communities with a source of
financing for economic development, housing rehabilitation, public facilities, and large-
scale physical development projects.

[4] The Neighborhood Stabilization Program was established for the purpose of stabilizing
communities that have suffered from housing foreclosures and abandonment. The first
phase of this program (NSP1) provided $3.92 billion in grant funds. The American
Recovery and Reinvestment Act of 2009 (Pub. L. No. 111-5) provided an additional $2
billion in NSP funds (referred to as NSP2) and changed several aspects of the program.
Later, the Dodd-Frank Wall Street Reform and Consumer Protection Act (Pub. L. No. 111-
203) provided an additional $1 billion in funding for the program (referred to as NSP3).

communities are defined by statute, as cities with populations greater than 50,000 people or urban counties with populations of 200,000 or more.

CDF also receives supplemental appropriations for its disaster recovery programs, which have varying periods of availability depending on the legislation. In addition, HUD officials said funds supporting NSP1 and NSP3 are mandatory and all CDBG funds are discretionary.

What Factors Affect the Size or Composition of the Carryover Balance?

During fiscal years 2007 through 2012, the size of the carryover balance in the CDF account ranged from approximately $16 billion to about $29 billion. As shown in figure 11, the obligated but unexpended portion of the balance remained fairly steady over the six year period. The unobligated portion peaked in 2008 and subsequently decreased for the remainder of the period.

Figure 11: Carryover Balances in the Community Development Fund, Fiscal Years 2007-2012

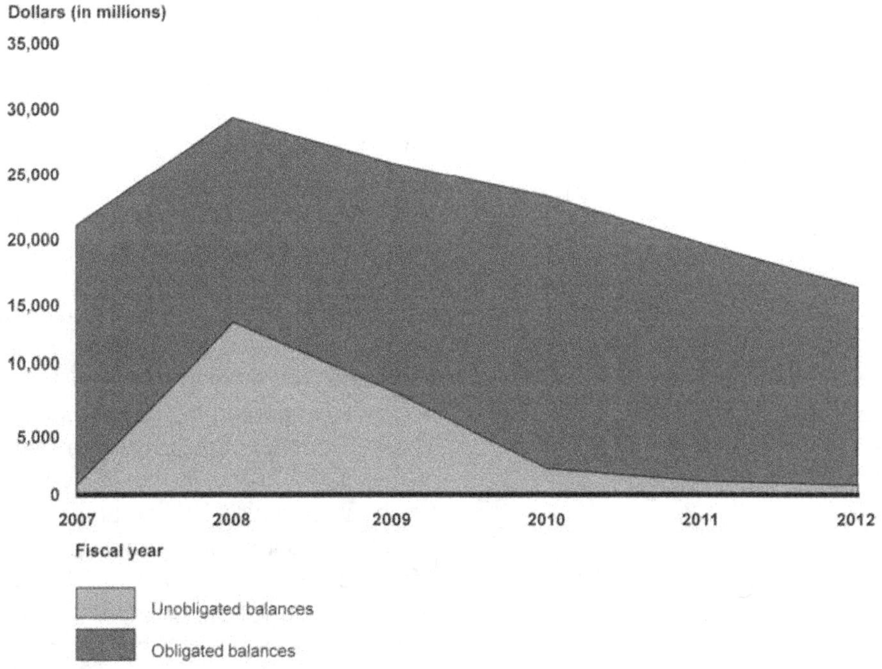

Source: GAO analysis of OMB MAX data.

Note: Balances shown here are end-of-year.

Supplemental appropriations contributed to larger than anticipated unobligated balances in fiscal years 2008 and 2009. Although officials said they make an effort to obligate supplemental appropriations quickly, if funds are received late in the fiscal year, it is more likely that a portion of the unobligated funds will carry over into the next fiscal year. For example, in 2008, HUD received a supplemental appropriation on September 30th to provide disaster relief to areas affected by hurricanes, floods, and other natural disasters. The timing of the appropriation led to a large increase in the unobligated balance carried over into the next fiscal year. In 2009, additional supplemental appropriations were enacted.

HUD officials said they typically obligate funds quickly; however, the rate of expenditure may be slow, resulting in a large obligated, unexpended balance from year to year. This is because once funds are obligated, the time it takes to expend funds depends on the rate at which grantees are drawing down their grant money. In the case of supplemental funds, the increased amount of grants may be a challenge for grantees to disburse. For example, HUD officials said that in one instance, a grantee that typically received a couple hundred thousand dollars per year received approximately $18 million in grant funds. Such a dramatic increase in the amount of grant funding posed administrative challenges for the grantee, which contributed to a slower spendout rate.

How Does the Agency Estimate and Manage Carryover Balances?

Estimates of carryover balances are determined through a review of prior year balances in the account. For example, when estimating the portion of the balance attributed to the traditional CDBG program, officials said they look at the composition of carryover balances from recent years, including whether the balances are composed of funds in their first year, second year, or third year of availability. They also consider historical rates of obligations and outlays. For the portion of the balance attributed to disaster recovery grants, it is more difficult to estimate carryover because estimating the timing and size of supplemental appropriations for disaster recovery are beyond the agency's control.

As shown in figure 12, actual unobligated balances were larger than estimated during fiscal years 2007 through 2012, with the largest difference occurring in 2008. Although the budget-year estimate of the unobligated balance for fiscal year 2007 was fairly close to the actual, the agency generally underestimated the amount of unobligated funds that would be carried over each year. For example, in 2008 and 2009, as discussed above, the agency unexpectedly received supplemental

appropriations that caused the actual balance to be considerably higher
than the previous estimates.

**Figure 12: Estimated vs. Actual Unobligated Balances in the Community
Development Fund, Fiscal Years 2007-2012**

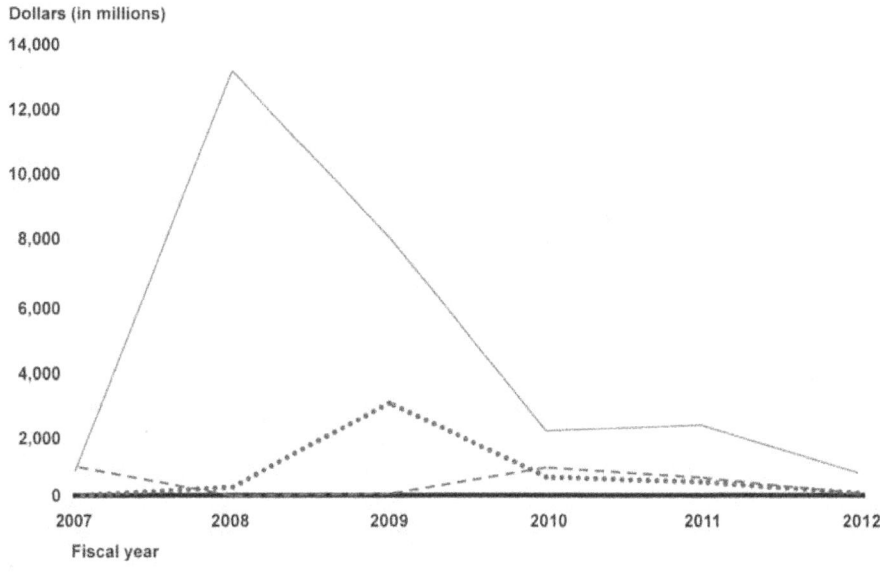

Dollars (in millions)

Fiscal year

——————— Actual unobligated balance

••••••• Estimated unobligated balance (CY)

– – – – Estimated unobligated balance (BY)

Source: GAO analysis of OMB data.

Note: Balances shown here are end-of-year.

Account Name:	Federal Housing Administration Mutual Mortgage Insurance (MMI) Capital Reserve Account
Agency:	Department of Housing and Urban Development
National Priority:	Mortgage Credit (Budget Subfunction 371)

What Mission and Goals Is the Account or Program Supporting?

The MMI Capital Reserve account supports the Federal Housing Administration's (FHA) Mutual Mortgage Insurance Fund (MMI Fund). Under the MMI Fund, FHA insures a variety of mortgages for home purchases and refinancing to meet the housing needs of traditionally underserved borrowers.[5] FHA has played a prominent role in the single-family mortgage market and accounted for more than 25 percent of the home purchase mortgages originated in fiscal year 2012.

Like other federal credit agencies, FHA estimates and re-estimates the net lifetime costs—known as credit subsidy costs—of the mortgages it insures. When the present value of estimated cash inflows (such as borrower insurance premiums) exceed the present value of expected cash outflows (such as insurance claims), negative subsidies are generated. These negative subsidies are held in the MMI Capital Reserve account as an unobligated balance. When FHA experiences unanticipated increases in estimated credit subsidy costs (upward re-estimates), balances in the MMI Capital Reserve account help to cover these increases.

What Are the Sources and Fiscal Characteristics of the Funding?

The MMI Capital Reserve account accumulates negative subsidies resulting from FHA's single-family mortgage insurance activities. It also earns interest and realizes gains on investment in nonmarketable Treasury securities. In the event the MMI Capital Reserve account is depleted, FHA is authorized to draw on permanent and indefinite budget authority to cover additional increases in estimated credit subsidy costs.

---

[5] FHA also insures reverse mortgages that permit persons 62 and older to convert their home equity into cash advances.

The MMI Capital Reserve account contains only mandatory funds, and those funds are available until expended.

What Factors Affect the Size or Composition of the Carryover Balance?

As shown in figure 13, carryover balances declined during the 6 years we reviewed, with a steep decline in 2009 and 2010. Because the spendout rate in this account is very quick, and in effect obligations are equivalent to outlays, nearly all of the carryover balances are unobligated.

Figure 13: Carryover Balance in the FHA-Mutual Mortgage Insurance Capital Reserve Account, Fiscal Years 2007-2012

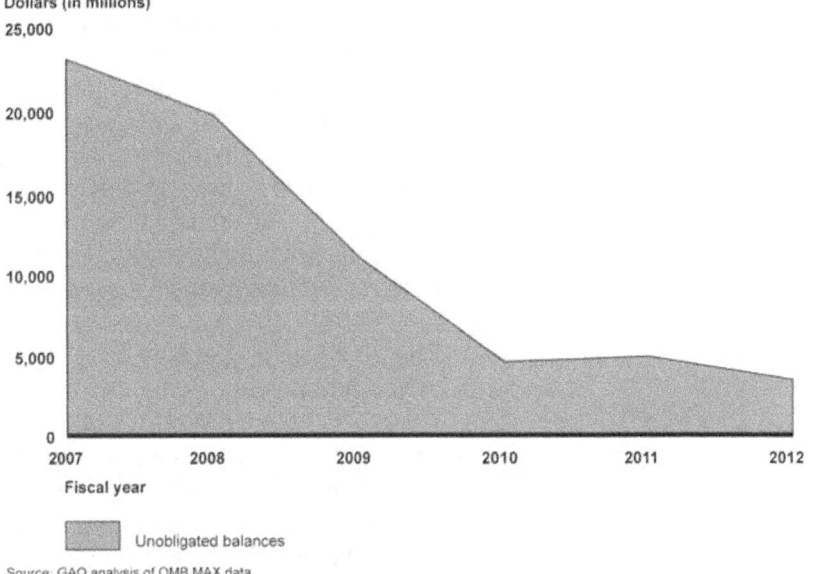

Source: GAO analysis of OMB MAX data.

Note: Balances shown here are end-of-year. In fiscal years 2007 through 2012, HUD reported negative obligated balances for the account. HUD officials said the negative balance represented outstanding receipts that had not yet been collected or fully processed by the end of the fiscal year. For presentation purposes, we do not show the obligated balance here.

The MMI Capital Reserve account maintains balances to cover unexpected insurance claim expenses, so when FHA experiences financial stress, the account balance decreases. For example, when the MMI Fund experiences higher-than-expected mortgage defaults (resulting in higher claims), there will be an upward re-estimate of credit subsidy costs. When there is an upward re-estimate, the MMI Capital Reserve account is the first source of funds used to cover the higher costs, thus lowering balances in the account. During the housing crisis that began in 2007, more pessimistic forecasts of economic conditions—house prices, in particular—resulted in higher projected insurance claims. As a result, balances in the MMI Capital Reserve account fell dramatically. From 2009 through 2012, FHA has submitted upward credit subsidy re-estimates ranging from about $6.8 to $10.5 billion annually. If upward re-estimates were to deplete the balance in the MMI Capital Reserve Account, FHA would need to draw on permanent, indefinite budget authority to have sufficient reserves for all future insurance claims on its existing portfolio.

How Does the Agency Estimate and Manage Carryover Balances?

The MMI Fund is reviewed from actuarial, financial and budgetary perspectives each year, which helps officials estimate carryover balances. From the actuarial perspective, FHA is statutorily required to ensure that the MMI Fund maintains a 2-percent capital ratio (discussed in more detail below). For its financial statements, FHA calculates the liability for loan guarantees, which represents the net present value of future cash flows on FHA's existing portfolio. From a budgetary perspective, FHA must follow the Federal Credit Reform Act of 1990, which requires the agency to estimate and re-estimate the net lifetime costs of the mortgages it insures.

The MMI Capital Reserve account holds funds to help FHA meet the statutory 2-percent capital ratio requirement for the MMI Fund and, as previously noted, maintains balances for unexpected claim expenses.[6] The capital ratio is defined as the MMI Fund's economic value divided by the total insurance-in-force.[7] The balance in the MMI Capital Reserve account is one component of the economic value, along with the balance in the MMI Financing Account (which maintains balances to cover

---

[6] The Omnibus Budget Reconciliation Act of 1990 (Pub. L. No. 101-508) required the Secretary of Housing and Urban Development to take steps to ensure that the MMI Fund attained a capital ratio of at least 2 percent by November 2000 and maintained at least a 2 percent ratio at all times thereafter.

[7] The economic value of the fund is the sum of existing capital resources plus the net present value of future cash flows. The unamortized insurance-in-force is generally understood as the initial insured loan balances. However, a legislative provision defines unamortized insurance-in-force as the remaining obligation on outstanding mortgages, a definition generally understood to mean the amortized insurance-in-force.

estimated credit subsidy costs) and the net present value of future cash flows. However, as a result of the economic downturn and housing crisis, the fund did not meet this requirement from 2009 through 2012. To help increase balances in the MMI Capital Reserve account and bring the MMI Fund back into compliance, FHA has implemented policy changes, including increases in borrower insurance premiums and enhanced underwriting requirements.

As shown in figure 14, actual unobligated balances were lower than originally estimated for all years. Current year estimates were very close for almost all years during the period. This shows that the agency's process for estimating unobligated balances assumed an accurate trend in most years, but tended to overestimate future balances, especially in fiscal year 2012.

Figure 14: Estimated vs. Actual Unobligated Balances in the FHA-Mutual Mortgage Insurance Capital Reserve Account, Fiscal Years 2007-2012

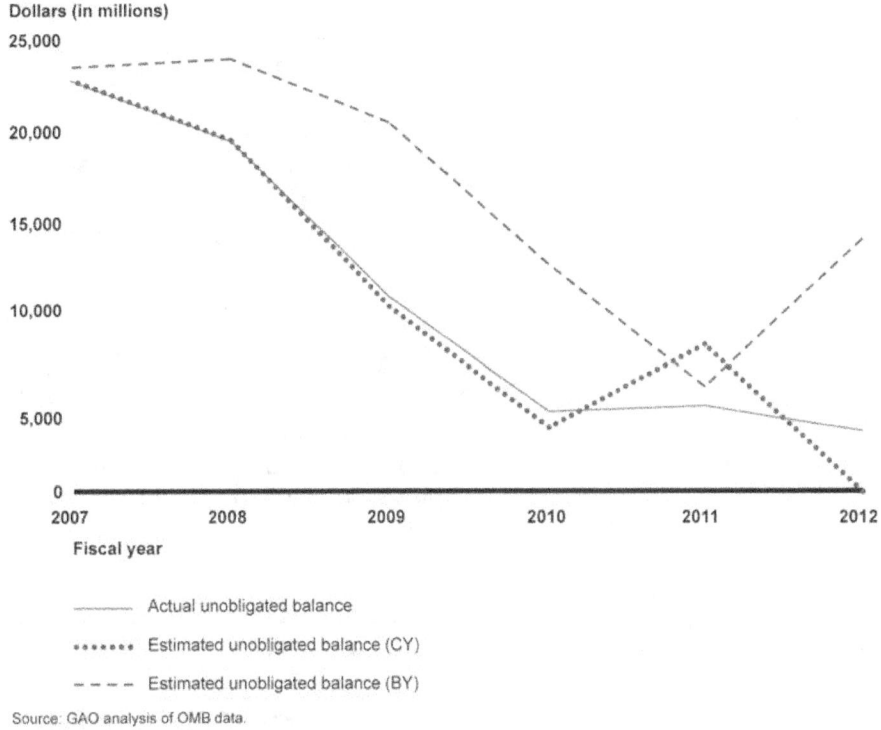

Source: GAO analysis of OMB data.

Note: Balances shown here are end-of-year.

Account Name: Homeless Assistance Grants (HAG)
Agency: Department of Housing and Urban Development
National Priority: Housing Assistance (Budget Subfunction 604)

What Mission and Goals Is the Account or Program Supporting?

The Homeless Assistance Grants (HAG) account funds two primary grant programs: the Continuum of Care program and the Emergency Solutions Grant program. The Continuum of Care program is HUD's largest and broadest targeted program to provide funds to address homelessness and the Emergency Solutions Grant Program includes funds for a variety of activities such as rapid re-housing. Grants through the Continuum of Care program are awarded through a national competition. An average of 87 percent of those funds per year goes to renew existing projects. The process to register, compete, and award grants is done on a calendar year basis and generally takes about seven months. The grant competition cycle begins after the agency receives a final annual appropriation. Once grants are awarded, funds are obligated and disbursed to grantees.

The 2009 Homeless Emergency Assistance and Rapid Transition to Rehousing Act (HEARTH)[8] resulted in several changes to HAG, including the consolidation of three grant programs[9] into the Continuum of Care program and allocation of funds to specific grant programs.

What are the Sources and Fiscal Characteristics of the Funding?

Funds in the HAG account are discretionary, provided through annual appropriations, and available for obligation for three years. In addition, in June 2008, the account received one multi-year supplemental appropriation of $50 million for aid to the State of Louisiana for the provision of 3,000 units of permanent supportive housing.[10]

---

[8] Pub. L. No. 111-22.

[9] The Continuum of Care program is currently composed of the (1) Shelter Plus Care, (2) Supportive Housing, and (3) Section 8 Moderate Rehabilitation Single Room Occupancy programs.

[10] Pub. L. No. 110-252.

What Factors Affect the Size or Composition of the Carryover Balance?

The carryover balance in the HAG account ranged from $4 billion to $5.6 billion during fiscal years 2007 through 2012. As shown in figure 15, unobligated balances remained steady over the six year period. In 2009, there was an increase in the obligated balance that subsequently decreased in later years.

Figure 15: Carryover Balances in the Homeless Assistance Grants Account, Fiscal Years 2007-2012

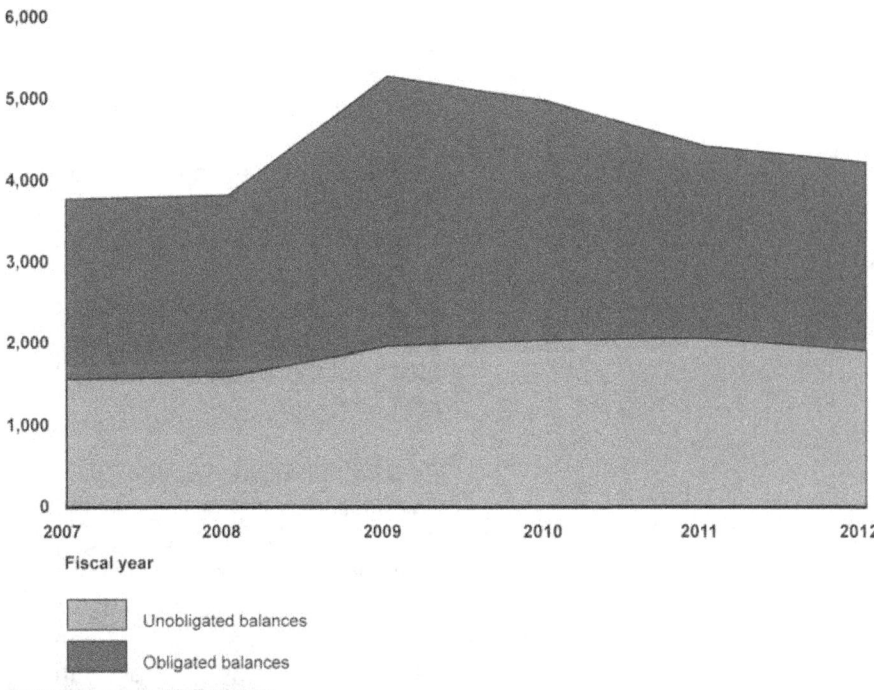

Source: GAO analysis of OMB MAX data.

Note: Balances shown here are end-of-year.

A portion of the unobligated balance results from the timing of the grant competition and award process, which is done by calendar year rather than fiscal year. For HAG, the typical grant competition cycle involves several phases. First, once the agency has received its annual appropriations, it then opens a program registration period. After the agency reviews registrations, it opens the grant application process. Following the final application review, grants are awarded at a later date during the current or next calendar year (likely during a new fiscal year).

At that point the available multi-year funds will be obligated. Because grant awards are typically made after the end of the fiscal year, unobligated balances are carried over from one fiscal year to the next.

Officials said the increase in the obligated, unexpended balance that occurred in 2009 and 2010 was the result of two events. In 2009, the account received $1.5 billion for HUD's Homelessness Prevention and Rapid Re-housing Program, which contributed to the increase in the obligated balance. In addition, the agency implemented a change in its process to review renewal grants. This change in process, which started in 2008, involved transitioning from a paper-based system to an electronic-based system. Officials said launching the new system caused a delay in awarding and disbursing grants, which resulted in an increased carryover balance.

How Does the Agency Estimate and Manage Carryover Balances?

Renewal grants account for the largest share of grant funding in the account and are typically funded before new grant applications are considered. Accordingly, HUD officials develop estimates of the account's carryover balance based on the historical rate of grant renewal from previous years. This helps the agency project the number of grants that will likely be renewed in the future, thereby informing HUD's estimate of the amount of funds that will be carried forward from one fiscal year to the next.

As shown in figure 16, from 2007 through 2010 actual unobligated balances were slightly higher than initial estimates. From 2009 through 2012, the actual unobligated balance remained fairly steady while agency estimates predicted more fluctuation. The largest difference between the estimated and actual unobligated balance was in 2012. Generally speaking, it appears that the agency's process for estimating unobligated balances was fairly accurate during the time period.

Figure 16: Estimated vs. Actual Unobligated Balances in the Homeless Assistance
Grants Account, Fiscal Years 2007-2012

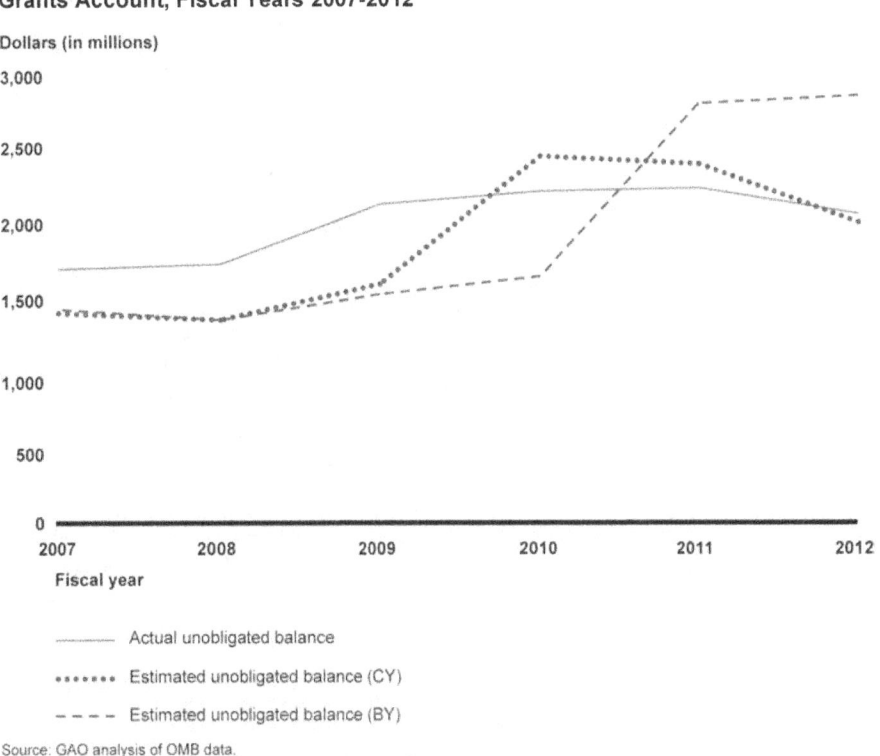

Source: GAO analysis of OMB data.

Note: Balances shown here are end-of-year.

Account Name:	Exchange Stabilization Fund (ESF)
Agency:	Department of the Treasury
National Priority:	International Financial Programs (Budget Subfunction 155)

What Mission and Goals Is the Account or Program Supporting?

The Exchange Stabilization Fund (ESF) account was established by the Gold Reserve Act of 1934, to be operated under the exclusive control of the Secretary of the Treasury with approval of the President. The primary purpose of the fund is to stabilize international financial markets, consistent with U.S. obligations in the International Monetary Fund (IMF). To carry out this purpose, the Secretary is authorized to purchase, sell, or deal in gold, foreign currencies, and other instruments of credit and securities. The ESF holds international reserve assets of the United States, including U.S. dollars, foreign exchange, and Special Drawing Rights (SDR).[11] If the maturity on an ESF loan or credit to a foreign entity or government will extend beyond six months, the President must give Congress a written statement that unique or emergency circumstances exist.

What Are the Sources and Fiscal Characteristics of the Funding?

The account received a $2 billion appropriation in 1934 when the fund was created. The Bretton Woods Agreements Act of 1945 directed the Treasury Secretary to pay $1.8 billion from the ESF to the IMF for the initial U.S. quota subscription in the IMF, thereby reducing ESF's appropriated amount to $200 million. Since that time, the major sources of the fund's income have been (1) gains (or losses) due to changes in exchange rates, (2) SDR allocations, and (3) earnings on investments held by the fund including interest earned on fund holdings of U.S. Government securities or interest on loans or credits to foreign governments. Amounts in the ESF, which is a public enterprise revolving

---

[11] The SDR is an international reserve asset and the unit of account of the IMF. Its value comprises a weighted average of the value of a basket of four currencies, of which the U.S. dollar has the largest share. Under the Special Drawing Rights Act of 1968, the Secretary of the Treasury may engage in SDR-related transactions including SDR allocations from the IMF, purchases of SDRs from other IMF member countries, and monetizations.

fund,[12] are available until expended and may not be used to pay administrative expenses.

What Factors Affect the Size or Composition of the Carryover Balance?

As shown in figure 17, the actual total carryover balance increased dramatically in fiscal year 2009 and remained at that level through fiscal year 2012. The obligated portion of the balance held steady in fiscal years 2007 through 2009. By the end of fiscal year 2010, the obligated portion of the total carryover balance had grown significantly. The unobligated balance stayed fairly steady throughout fiscal years 2007 to 2012 with the exception of a dramatic spike in fiscal year 2009.

---

[12] A public enterprise revolving fund is a type of revolving fund that conducts cycles of businesslike operations, mainly with the public, in which it charges for the sale of products or services and uses the proceeds to finance its spending, usually without requirement for annual appropriations. Most government corporations are financed by public enterprise funds.

**Figure 17: Carryover Balances in the Exchange Stabilization Fund, Fiscal Years
2007-2012**

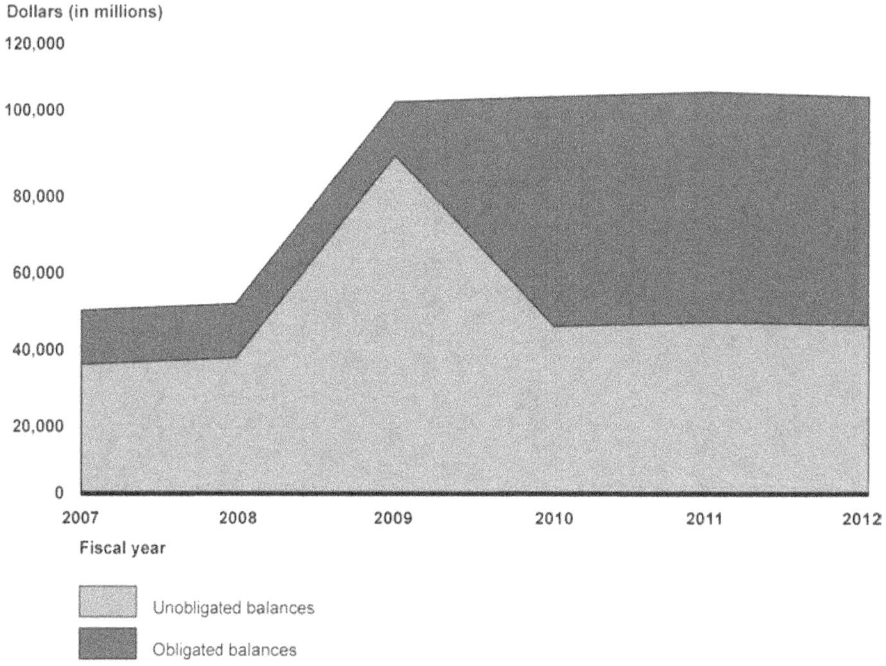

Source: GAO analysis of OMB MAX data

Note: Balances shown here are end-of-year.

Treasury officials said the largest single factor affecting the obligated
balance is attributed to changes made to ESF's budgetary reporting in
fiscal year 2010. According to Treasury officials, prior to fiscal year 2010,
the U.S. Standard General Ledger (USSGL) did not support the
budgetary transactions of the ESF, thereby making it impossible to do
ESF reporting using government-wide automated standards. The USSGL
Board established a standard ledger account specifically for the ESF as a
step toward correcting the budgetary reporting. Treasury's
implementation of this reporting change resulted in significant
adjustments to ESF account balances and caused the size of the
obligated balance to grow as a share of the total carryover balance in
fiscal years 2010 through 2012.

The spike in the unobligated balance in 2009 is almost entirely attributed
to approximately $50 billion of new SDR allocations and one transaction
that occurred over a one-month period. Pursuant to decisions made by

the IMF membership, the IMF provided general and special SDR allocations[13] to its members, including approximately $47.3 billion to the United States. As noted earlier, SDRs are held in the ESF. Treasury officials said the general allocation was an important element of the response to the global economic crisis. Further, they said the IMF general allocation provided an additional reserve buffer for IMF member countries that was critical to stopping the capital drain from emerging market countries and restoring global market confidence. In addition, Treasury monetized $3 billion of its ESF SDRs in a transaction authorized under the Special Drawing Rights Act.[14]

How Does the Agency Estimate and Manage Carryover Balances?

Treasury officials said they do not estimate carryover or unobligated balances for the ESF as they do in other accounts (e.g., salaries and expenses). The balances represent investments and the unobligated balance is calculated from ESF's balance sheet: assets minus liabilities.

Account estimates reported in the President's Budget each fiscal year are based on projected net interest earnings on ESF assets. The estimates are subject to considerable variance, depending on changes in the amount and composition of assets and the interest rates applied to investments. The estimates make no attempt to forecast gains or losses on SDR valuation or foreign currency valuation.

As shown in figure 18, the nearly $50 billion of SDR-related transactions in fiscal year 2009 led to an actual unobligated balance in the ESF that was much larger than was estimated in fiscal year 2007 when the President's fiscal year 2009 budget was developed. Moreover, these

---

[13] Under its Articles of Agreement, the IMF may allocate SDRs to member countries in proportion to their IMF quotas. General allocations of SDRs have to be based on a long-term global need to supplement existing reserve assets. An amendment to the Articles of Agreement in August 2009 provided for a one-time special allocation. The purpose of the amendment was to enable all IMF members to participate in the SDR system on an equitable basis.

[14] When the Secretary of the Treasury monetizes SDRs, he is converting SDRs (an international reserve asset) into more readily usable US dollars. The Secretary issues SDR certificates to the Federal Reserve banks against SDRs held by the ESF. In turn, the Federal Reserve banks purchase these SDR certificates with US dollars. The US dollar proceeds of the monetization are held in the ESF and may be used only for financing the acquisition of more SDRs or for other statutorily authorized purposes of the ESF.

transactions had a direct impact on Treasury's estimates of the
unobligated balance in subsequent years. Treasury officials said the
general timing of those transactions was concurrent with the agency's
development of its fiscal year 2010 mid-year estimate and fiscal year
2011 budget-year estimate for the account. Generally, in proportion to the
size of the account, Treasury's process for estimating the unobligated
balance was relatively accurate.

**Figure 18: Estimated vs. Actual Unobligated Balances in the Exchange Stabilization
Fund, Fiscal Years 2007-2012**

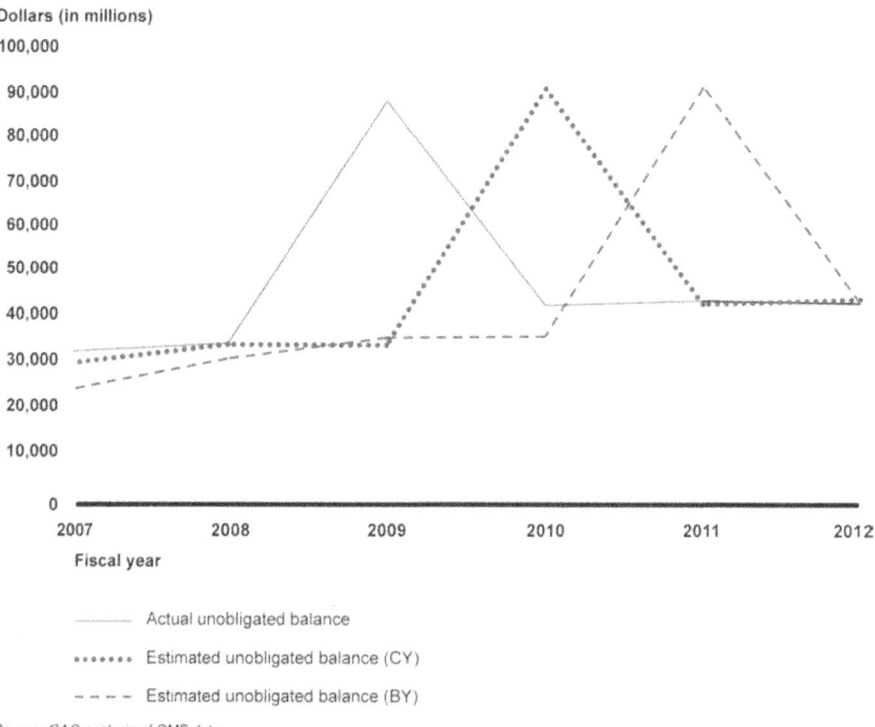

Source: GAO analysis of OMB data.

Note: Balances shown here are end-of-year.

GAO-13-798 Budget Issues

Account Name: Government Sponsored Enterprise (GSE)
Preferred Stock Purchase Agreements
Agency: Department of the Treasury
National Priority: Mortgage Credit (Budget Subfunction 371)

What Mission and Goals Is the Account or Program Supporting?

In 2008, the Housing and Economic Recovery Act (HERA)[15] established
the Federal Housing Finance Agency (FHFA). FHFA placed two
Government Sponsored Enterprises (GSE)[16]—the Federal National
Mortgage Association (Fannie Mae) and the Federal Home Loan
Mortgage Corporation (Freddie Mac)—into conservatorship. Treasury
then entered into agreements with Fannie Mae and Freddie Mac to
provide capital through investments in senior preferred stock to ensure
that each company maintained a positive net worth. Treasury disburses
funds to the GSEs if, at the end of any quarter, the liabilities of either GSE
exceed its assets.

Amendments to the agreements in 2009 changed the maximum allowable
funding commitment, which is reflected in the unobligated balances.
Initially in 2008, Treasury was authorized to purchase up to $100 billion of
securities and investments in each GSE for a total of $200 billion. The
first amendment in May 2009 increased the allowable investment level to
$200 billion for each GSE. In December 2009, the second amendment
changed the investment level so it was based on a formulaic cap that
would automatically adjust upwards quarterly by the cumulative amount of
any losses realized by either GSE and downward by the cumulative
amount of any gains, but not below $200 billion.[17]

---

[15] Pub. L. No. 110-289.

[16] GSEs are federally chartered, privately owned financial institutions designed to facilitate
the flow of investment funds to specific economic sectors. GSEs typically receive financing
from private investment, and the credit markets perceive that GSEs have implied federal
financial backing. GSEs issue capital stock and short- and long-term debt instruments,
issue mortgage-backed securities, fund designated activities, and collect fees for
guarantees and other services.

[17] Beginning on January 1, 2013, the remaining funding commitment is fixed and will
remain available to be drawn per the terms of the agreement.

What Are the Sources and Fiscal Characteristics of the Funding?

HERA established temporary authority for the GSE Purchase Agreements account and granted the Treasury Secretary temporary authority to purchase obligations and securities. The Secretary has complete discretion over the terms, conditions, and amounts of the purchases, provided that he or she (1) designates the actions as necessary, (2) takes specific considerations into account, and (3) reports on these matters to Congress. Any funds expended under this authority are deemed as appropriated in such sums as needed.[18]

What Factors Affect the Size or Composition of the Carryover Balance?

As shown in figure 19, the actual total carryover balance in the account grew significantly from fiscal years 2007 through 2009 and subsequently declined through fiscal year 2012.

The spendout rate in this account is very quick, which results in the agency reporting no obligated balance in the account by year-end. In effect, the actual payments to the GSEs are equal to the amount of obligations incurred and outlays reported in the President's Budget Appendix. Treasury officials said the unobligated portion of the balance represents the cash balance in the account.

---

[18] As part of the purchase agreements with the GSEs, Treasury was entitled to receive cumulative cash dividends on the senior preferred stock from the date of initial issuance through December 31, 2012. These amounts were deposited in the General Fund.

Figure 19: Carryover Balances in the GSE Purchase Agreements Account, Fiscal Years 2007-2012

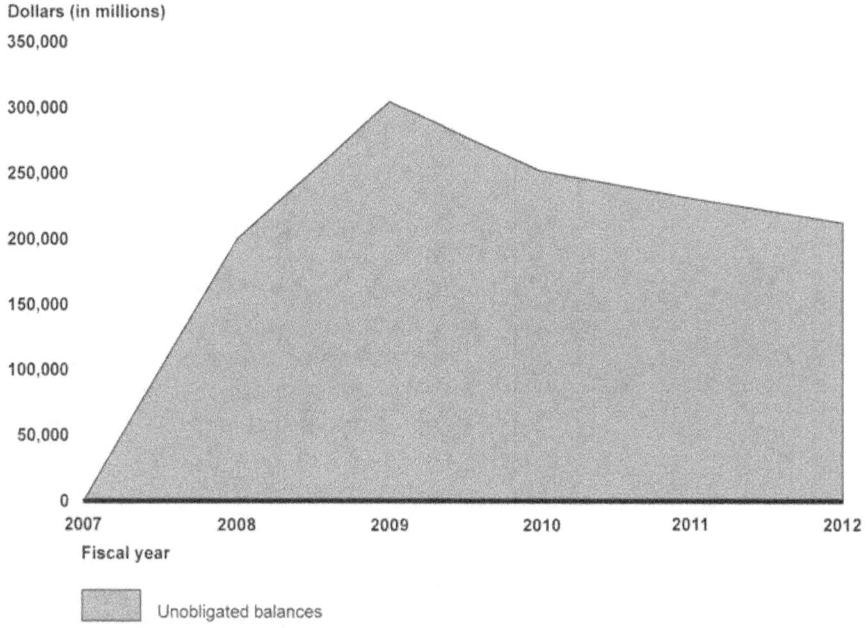

Source: GAO analysis of OMB MAX data.

Note: Balances shown here are end-of-year. The account was established in 2008 under HERA, which means that there were no balances to report prior to 2008.

The carryover balance is generally driven by the size of the apportionment[19] to the account and the amount of purchases made by the account. For example, the account started with a $200 billion balance in budget authority when it was created under HERA in 2008. In 2009, the maximum allowable funding commitment was increased by an additional $200 billion for the account. Treasury also made its first payments to the GSEs equal to $95.6 billion. As shown in figure 19, this translated into an unobligated balance of $304.4 billion at the end of fiscal year 2009. Prior

---

[19] Apportionment is the action by which the Office of Management and Budget (OMB) distributes amounts available for obligation, including budgetary reserves established pursuant to law, in an appropriation or fund account. An apportionment divides amounts available for obligation by specific time periods (usually quarters), activities, projects, objects, or a combination thereof. The amounts so apportioned limit the amount of obligations that may be incurred.

GAO-13-798 Budget Issues

to making payments to the GSEs, Treasury received an apportionment of its budget authority from OMB at the beginning of the fiscal year for the unobligated balance brought forward in the account.

The gradual decline in the unobligated balance reflects Treasury's subsequent payments to the GSEs in fiscal years 2010 through 2012, bringing the balance down to $212.5 billion by the close of fiscal year 2012.[20]

How Does the Agency Estimate and Manage Carryover Balances?

Budget year estimates of the unobligated balance are derived from the estimated draws on the account from year to year. To do this, Treasury annually prepares a series of long-range forecasts to determine the estimated amount of contingent liability to the GSEs under the purchase agreements. These projections inform the agency's estimation of payments to the GSEs for a given year. Based on the size of the estimated payments, Treasury estimates the amount of budget authority that will be carried over into the next year. By the time the agency develops current year estimates, agency officials said they typically know what the size of the payment request will be, thereby contributing to a more accurate estimate of the unobligated balance that is carried forward. This informs apportionment decisions to ensure there are sufficient funds to cover the payments to the GSEs.

As shown in figure 20, there were no estimated unobligated balances in fiscal years 2007 through 2009. This is attributed to the timing of the President's budget preparation for each of those years, and to the creation of the Purchase Agreement account. The account was established after the enactment of HERA in 2008, which meant that the account's estimates were issued for the first time in the President's fiscal year 2010 budget. Similarly, there were no actual unobligated balances to report prior to 2008. During fiscal years 2010 through 2012, Treasury's estimates of the unobligated balance in the account were slightly lower than, but fairly close to, the actual balance at year-end. In proportion to the size of this account, this suggests that the agency's estimation process for this account was relatively accurate in those years.

---

[20] Subsequent to 2009, payments to the GSEs were smaller: $52.6 billion in 2010, $20.8 billion in 2011, and $18.5 billion in 2012.

Figure 20: Estimated vs. Actual Unobligated Balances in the GSE Purchase Agreements Account, Fiscal Years 2007-2012

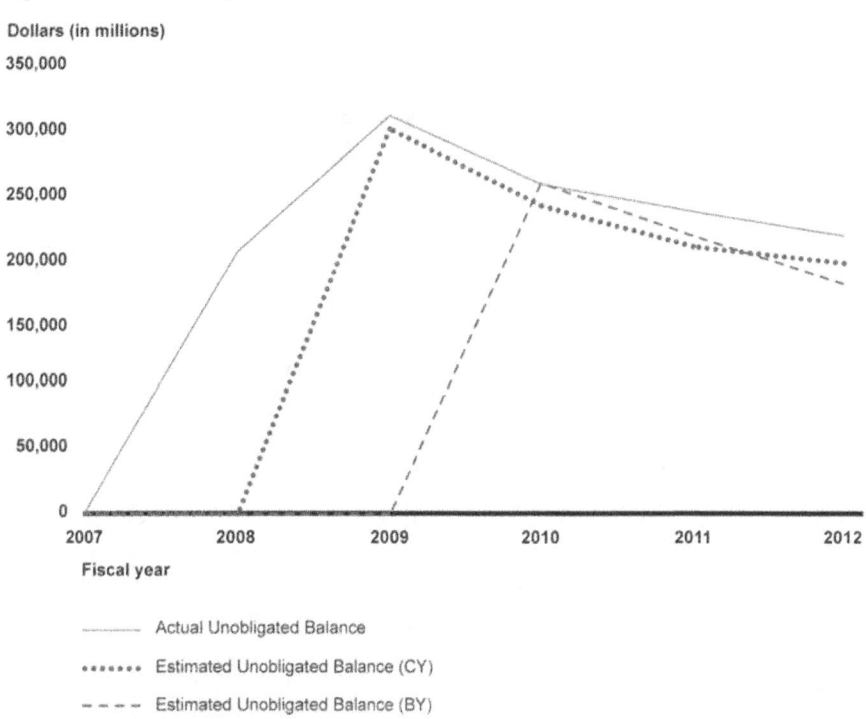

Dollars (in millions)

Fiscal year

———— Actual Unobligated Balance

•••••• Estimated Unobligated Balance (CY)

– – – – Estimated Unobligated Balance (BY)

Source: GAO analysis of OMB data.

Note: Balances shown here are end-of-year. Because the account was created in 2008, its budget estimates were issued for the first time in the President's fiscal year 2010 budget.

Appendix IV: Comments from the Department of Health and Human Services

DEPARTMENT OF HEALTH & HUMAN SERVICES

OFFICE OF THE SECRETARY

Assistant Secretary for Legislation
Washington, DC 20201

SEP 6 2013

Carol Henn, Assistant Director
Strategic Issues
U.S. Government Accountability Office
441 G Street NW
Washington, DC 20548

Dear Ms. Henn,

Attached are comments on the U.S. Government Accountability Office's (GAO) report entitled, "Budget Issues: Key Questions to Consider When Evaluating Balances in Federal Accounts" (GAO-13-798).

The Department appreciates the opportunity to review this report prior to publication.

Sincerely,

Jim R. Esquea
Assistant Secretary for Legislation

Attachment

**GENERAL COMMENTS OF THE DEPARTMENT OF HEALTH AND HUMAN
SERVICES (HHS) ON THE GOVERNMENT ACCOUNTABILITY OFFICE'S (GAO)
DRAFT REPORT ENTITLED, "BUDGET ISSUES: KEY QUESTIONS TO CONSIDER
WHEN EVALUATING BALANCES IN FEDERAL ACCOUNTS" (GAO-13-798)**

The Department appreciates the opportunity to review and comment on this draft report.

HHS believes it is important to note that GAO chose to audit only a select number of accounts,
which may or may not be representative of all government accounts with carry forward balances,
so any conclusions drawn from the report may not apply across the board to all multi-year or no-
year accounts. GAO chose to audit only the HHS PHSSEF fund, which has complexities and
authorities that may differ from other Federal accounts. While the report acknowledges some of
these complexities, such as the impact of disasters and supplemental appropriations upon spend
rates, it may not be a correct approach to look at trends over time to overcome these complexities
when trying to determine spend rates or reasons for fluctuations in spend rates.

1

Appendix V: Glossary of Budget Terms

Appropriation: Budget authority to incur obligations and to make payments from the Treasury for specified purposes. An appropriation act is the most common means of providing appropriations; however, authorizing and other legislation itself may provide appropriations.

> **Annual appropriation:** An act appropriating funds enacted annually by Congress to provide budget authority to incur obligations and make payments from the Treasury for specified purposes.

> **Supplemental appropriation:** An act appropriating funds in addition to those already enacted in an annual appropriation act. Supplemental appropriations provide additional budget authority usually in cases where the need for funds is too urgent to be postponed until enactment of the regular appropriation bill. Supplemental appropriations may sometimes include items not appropriated in the regular bills due to a lack of timely authorizations.

Availability: Budget authority that is available for incurring new obligations.

Budget authority: Authority provided by federal law to enter into financial obligations that will result in immediate or future outlays involving federal government funds.

Budget function: The functional classification system is a way of grouping budgetary resources so that all budget authority and outlays of on-budget and off-budget federal entities and tax expenditures can be presented according to the national needs being addressed. National needs are grouped in 17 broad areas to provide a coherent and comprehensive basis for analyzing and understanding the budget.

Budget year: A term used in the budget formulation process to refer to the fiscal year for which the budget is being considered, that is, with respect to a session of Congress, the fiscal year of the government that starts on October 1 of the calendar year in which that session of Congress begins.

Carryover balance (unexpended balance): The sum of the obligated and unobligated balances.

Commitment: An administrative reservation of allotted funds, or of other funds, in anticipation of their obligation.

Continuing resolution: An appropriation act that provides budget authority for federal agencies, specific activities (or both) to continue in operation when Congress and the President have not completed action on the regular appropriation acts by the beginning of the fiscal year.

Current year: A term used in the budget formulation process to refer to the fiscal year immediately preceding the budget year under consideration.

Deobligate: A cancellation or downward adjustment of previously incurred obligations made by an agency. Deobligated funds may be reobligated within the period of availability of the appropriation.

Discretionary spending: Outlays from budget authority that is provided in, and controlled by, appropriations acts.

Expended funds: Funds that have actually been disbursed or outlaid.

Mandatory spending: Budget authority that is provided in laws other than appropriation acts and the outlays that result from such budget authority. Mandatory spending includes entitlement authority (for example, Food Stamp, Medicare and veterans' pension programs), payment of interest on the public debt, and nonentitlements such as payments to states from Forest Service receipts.

Obligated balance (obligated funds): The amount of obligations already incurred for which payment has not yet been made. Technically, the obligated balance is the unliquidated obligations. Budget authority that is available for a fixed period expires at the end of its period of availability, but the obligated balance of the budget authority remains available to liquidate obligations for five additional fiscal years. At the end of the fiscal year, the account is closed and any remaining balance is canceled. Budget authority available for an indefinite period may be canceled, and its account closed if (1) it is specifically rescinded by law or (2) the head of the agency concerned (or the President) determines that the purposes for which the appropriation was made have been carried out and disbursements have not been made from the appropriation for 2 consecutive years.

Obligation: An obligation is a definite commitment that creates a legal liability of the government for the payment of goods and services ordered or received, or a legal duty on the part of the United States that could mature into a legal liability by virtue of actions of another party.

Spendout rate: The rate at which budget authority becomes outlays in a fiscal year. It is usually presented as an annual percentage.

Unexpended balance: The sum of the obligated and unobligated balances.

Unobligated balance (unobligated funds): The portion of obligational authority that has not yet been obligated. For an appropriation account that is available for a fixed period, the budget authority expires after the period of availability ends but its unobligated balance remains available for 5 additional fiscal years for recording and adjusting obligations properly chargeable to the appropriations period of availability. For example, an expired, unobligated balance remains available until the account is closed to record previously unrecorded obligations or to make upward adjustments in previously under recorded obligations (such as contract modifications properly within scope of the original contract). At the end of the fifth fiscal year, the account is closed and any remaining balance is canceled. For a no-year account, the unobligated balance is carried forward indefinitely until (1) specifically rescinded by law or (2) the head of the agency concerned (or the President) determines that the purposes for which the appropriation was made have been carried out and disbursements have not been made from the appropriation for 2 consecutive years.

Appendix VI: GAO Contact and Staff Acknowledgments

GAO Contact	Susan J. Irving, (202) 512-6806 or irvings@gao.gov.
Staff Acknowledgments	In addition to the contact named above, Carol M. Henn, Assistant Director, Leah Q. Nash and Mary C. Diop made major contributions to this report. Also contributing to this report were Rob Gebhart, Tara Jayant, Kate Lenane, Felicia Lopez, John Mingus Jr., Robert Robinson, and Cindy Saunders. In addition, the following individuals provided programmatic expertise: Marcia Crosse, Shana R. Deitch, Cheryl Goodman, Marshall Hamlett, Vondalee R. Hunt, Thomas Melito, Paul Schmidt, Mathew J. Scire, William B. Shear, Andrea P. Smith, Bruce Thomas, and Steve Westley.